Praise for Host of Memories . . .

"I couldn't put down Peter Rupert Lighte's *Host of Memories* until I had finished it. Every chapter is filled with a rich assortment of characters that he has met, loved, and learned from during an adventurous life. I hope he continues this project of recording memories in his elegant prose for us to read more."

—Alison Klayman, director, *Ai Weiwei: Never Sorry*

"The author's warmhearted, positive temperament shines through this eminently readable collection of tiny stories that together form an unusual autobiography about an unusual life lived in many interesting locations around the world. With enviable 'total recall' of the big and small moments in his life, Peter Lighte illuminates personal encounters and family history with quirky humor and elegant style. An entrancing book."

—Judith Weir, composer

"An engaging collection of anecdotes, *Host of Memories* begins with tales from the author's childhood in New York and Florida, and continues through his discovery of ancient Chinese philosophy and history in university, and his unlikely transformation from Chinese scholar to distinguished international banker. The chapters dance from New York to London, Tokyo, Beijing, Sydney, Hong Kong, and many points in between. With a lively sense of humor and no holds barred, his stories reveal the roots and development of a man deeply appreciative of family and friends, who shines as a wonderful storyteller and an exceptional human being."

—Tom Gorman
Chairman and editor-in-chief, *Fortune China*

"Peter Lighte has written a charming memoir—Proustian in detail but much easier to enjoy. It is a wonderful story of a life well-lived. Don't miss its erudite musings endowed with charm, thoughtfulness, detail, and delight."

—Sybil Shainwald, **women's advocate**

"As in his first book, *Pieces of China*, Lighte's sharp eye for details creates vivid pictures, whether of his childhood days in Florida and New York or in the prime of life in London. With a supporting cast of colorful and sometimes cheeky relatives, chance acquaintances who become adopted relatives, and others who are swept into oddball scenes, Lighte tells stories that are often funny, frequently touching, and always tied together by his irreverent perspective, empathy, and quick wit."

—Timothy Massad
Lawyer, Washington, DC

"Peter Rupert Lighte's stories remind me of those of Gerald Durrell, one of my favorite read-aloud authors."

—Melanie Clarke
Executive director of the Princeton Symphony Orchestra

"In this touching and insightful memoir, Lighte gracefully weaves a tapestry of tart anecdotes and sweet tales about the characters (significant and otherwise) who shaped his life. It's poignant, funny, and achingly sad—often all at once."

—Jenny Bowen, CEO of Half the Sky Foundation and
author of *Wish You Happy Forever*

"A little boy is so uncomfortable at a family dinner that he pushes his shoe into the center of the elegantly set table. Decades later, he gathers the relatives together to his own table—his own telling of their stories. Here the host of memories travels back and forth in time. With a keen sense of humor and detail, he makes us enjoy Aunt Marcy, a Hindu festival opening a textile factory in North Carolina, and a quirky Princeton doyenne, with all the sillinesses, misjudgments, and vulnerabilities of being alive."

-—Miriam Peskowitz
New York Times bestselling author of *The Daring Book for Girls*

"*Host of Memories* is an utterly charming book, weaving together kosher rituals in New York City, nights at the opera, draft dodging, quirky professors, sexual awakening, and China in the first years after its opening. The vignettes—perfect bedtime reading—resonate with universal themes, above all the love, strength, and eccentricity of an extended Jewish family. Lighte's aunts, cousins, grandparents, and step-relatives of all sorts are drawn with a warmth and affection that implants them in our own memories."

—Anne-Marie Slaughter
President/CEO of the New America Foundation, professor emerita at Princeton University, and former director of Policy Planning for the US Department of State

"This memoir deftly covers a remarkable range of changes in American society over the twentieth century through rites of passage—adolescence, divorce, death, and sexual awakening—as played out in family and academia. . . . Throughout, the hurly-burly of the author's personal existence reflects the dramatic cultural transformations surrounding him. And yet patterns emerged, revealing not only that young Peter felt life deeply but that his formative years never stopped informing him."

—William B. Russel
Dean emeritus of the Graduate School, Princeton University

HOST OF MEMORIES

Also by Peter Rupert Lighte:

Pieces of China

HOST OF MEMORIES

Tales of Inevitable Happenstance

Peter Rupert Lighte

Acausal Books

PRINCETON, NEW JERSEY

Published by:
Acausal Books
27 Haslet Avenue
Princeton, NJ 08540
www.acausalbooks.com

Editors: Lora Lisbon, Ellen Kleiner
Book design and production: Angela Werneke

First Edition

Proceeds from the sale of this book benefit Half the Sky Foundation

Printed in the United States of America

Publisher's Cataloging-in-Publication Data

Lighte, Peter Rupert.
    Host of memories : tales of inevitable happenstance / by Peter Rupert Lighte. —Princeton, NJ : Acausal Books, c2015.

        p. ; cm.

    ISBN: 978-0-9912529-7-8 (paperback)
    ISBN: 978-0-9912529-6-1 (eBook)
    Summary: The author writes with empathy of family, upheaval, learning, synchronicity, Princeton, home, and other memories that crowd his elastic life. He is convinced we all share a world alive with rhythm and complexity.—Publisher

    1. Autobiographical memory. 2. Episodic memory. 3. Memory.
    4. Jungian psychology. 5. Causation. 6. Coincidence. 7. Cycles.
    8. Autobiography. I. Title.

BF378.A87 L54 2015   2013956448
153.1/2—dc23   1501

1 3 5 7 9 10 8 6 4 2

For my daughters, Hattie and Tillie
and loving women along the Way

ACKNOWLEDGMENTS

UNKNOWINGLY IN THE THRALL of the passive voice, I consistently distanced myself from direct participation in the very tales I had asked Carol Wood to proofread. Faced with her undeniable findings, I set out to reenter life, no longer willing to be an absentee storyteller.

Gouri Mukherjee transformed himself into a mentoring editor from a J. P. Morgan colleague. He projected his brand of courtly rigor onto my brand of chaos, meshing his concern for my stories with respect for my spirit.

Enlisting Jeff Hartsough's help in the preparation of this book enhanced the pleasure of the endeavor. A soaring sinologist and dear godson, he not only scrutinized the manuscript with laser-like intensity but made nonsense of my claim to be a semicolon expert. I happily defer to him.

After dealing remotely with Lora Lisbon and Ellen Kleiner of Blessingway Authors' Services, I had great fun pitching up on their doorstep in Santa Fe. Over time, Lora gave me the informed courage to take an ax to unwieldy stories and Ellen took care that I scrubbed up well in print.

Angela Werneke, the designer of this book, through fonts, hexagrams, and color, helped me to better explain myself.

Jan Kline, my stepsister, read a difficult story and was graciously supportive of its inclusion in this book.

Alice Neufeld Elman, childhood friend and radiant first crush, generously read drafts of these stories, offering strategic insights into their flow. I am particularly indebted to her for guiding the creation of "Between the Acts."

Long ago, I had the pleasure of escorting Madeleine Fuchs Holzer, her arm in a sling, from the principal's office to Mrs. Kraf's class on her very first day at P. S. 90. Madeleine was a gentle and keen reader of my manuscript.

After reading a draft, Stephen Williams, Shelter Island friend and writer, offhandedly commented on the loving women who had crowded my life. Thanks to him, I was able to take pleasure in the obvious.

Beth Witherell, editor-in-chief of the *Writings of Henry D. Thoreau* and friend from our Princeton days, cast her sharp eye over the manuscript. Not only did I benefit from her literary insights, but the experience helped us pleasurably to reconnect.

Matias Cava, a young pal from Hay Beach, asked me to read a superb and learned chapter of his work in progress. I screwed up my courage, returned the favor, and benefited immensely from his insights.

Marion Morgenthal, a colleague and Bronx Science classmate, caused me to think about the differences between *that* and *which* on bank time.

Bert Lies and Rosina Yue never thought it odd that I wanted to know what kind of car Carl Gustav Jung drove; they helped me find out.

I came to life at Princeton University and in its town. Amongst the many personalities who fostered my transformation were three stars: the late Professor F. W. Mote, the late Mrs. Janet Cottier, and Jim Conte—a most unlikely troika. I dearly salute them.

Never complacent, I count myself lucky that Julian Grant—we are newlyweds—continues to see beyond my "late Henry James prose."

CONTENTS

INTRODUCTION

AFTER READING A FEW of the following stories about my childhood, my friend Muki wondered about my powers of recall. At first, I credited my ability to conjure up the past with precision to years of writing in diaries. But since I never consulted these diaries while recollecting the past for this book of tales, I reckoned that my memories were stored elsewhere.

One evening, on the train home to Princeton from New York City, I wrestled with my notion of time. To be sure, I did not live in the past; nor could I say that I lived only in the present, periodically recalling the past. I wondered if time somehow surrounded me. Then, while looking into the soaring great room of my house, my eyes lit upon a white figurine of Lin Biao seated in a porcelain armchair, and I was immediately in the Dirt Market of Beijing, having just bargained with a shopkeeper to split up the pair—I didn't want Chairman Mao.

I strolled around the living room, gauging the intensity of recollections triggered by my encounters with its materials and objects. The cork floor conjured up Alison, the builder of the house, whom I had known as a student. The Torah pointers hanging on a Chinese brush rack evoked a trip my mother had taken to Jerusalem and my own daughters' bat mitzvahs in Beijing. When I stopped before a large wooden ox near the fireplace, I recalled Vietnam. While lingering, I even remembered taking a terrible fall in a Saigon bathtub on a business trip. I then sat down in the room now brimming with time, crowded with many of the people in this book. There was no need to look over my shoulder to be in the past; there it was, arrayed before me. And rather than viewing a panorama of events that might pass for happenstance, I began to discern patterns amongst them, prompting an awareness that dissolved any suspicion of either chance or fate being at play in my life. Smiling, I flashed onto the White Queen's remark to Alice in Lewis Carroll's *Through the Looking-Glass:* "It's a poor sort of memory that only works backwards."

As a hospitable host in this room, I will give a guided tour of its interior, beginning with a story about Aunt Marcy, my mother's elder sister, who made my childhood safe. Without her in my room of time and happenstance, my mother's gift of wisdom might have been lost on me, muddled by the drama of my childhood.

WILLY'S GIRL

As an infant, I was taken in a basket aboard a Pan Am Clipper to New York from Florida to visit my maternal grandfather, Willy Simon. I was a chubby baby and had already been nicknamed Sidney Greenstreet, after the "Fat Man" in *The Maltese Falcon*, but my grandfather called me his canary because I always seemed to be singing. In black-and-white photos of the two of us, he appears gaunt due to age and emphysema, hardly the youthful man in our earlier family movies.

In the 1920s, Willy's elder daughters, Birdie and Marcy, were married within two years of each other, and both weddings were filmed by professional crews. While the styles of the two events were radically different, my grandfather appears in white tie for both. Looking dashing and dignified, nearly six feet six inches tall and sporting a jaunty mustache, he is in his prime. In one of the films, he is both playful with his younger children, one of whom is my mother, and bold, planting a big kiss on my grandmother's lips. He seems to be the quintessential new American, a Jewish immigrant grabbing life with both hands and turning his back on a world that did not want him.

Willy became an early car owner in New York City by winning a Model T in a raffle, a fact I discovered a lifetime later while driving with Aunt Marcy. Stopped at a red light, she shouted out to an old man crossing before us, "Aaron, is that you?" Indeed, it was the chauffeur my grandfather had "won" along with the Ford, since it had been assumed that people did not know how to drive in those dawning days of motoring.

As my grandfather prospered, the quality of his cars improved, but only one became iconic—a Packard with sleek running boards and silver vases mounted inside, seen even in faded photographs. Because Aunt Marcy was the first driver in the family, she naturally took charge of the family car.

Although my grandfather worked endless hours at Simon and Werner's, his East Harlem kosher poultry market, he still customarily closed the business before sundown on Fridays in recognition of the Sabbath. After locking the massive doors over which hung a sign depicting a gigantic chicken, he would make his way to a neighborhood Turkish bath to prepare himself for the houseful of company awaiting his arrival home for the ritual meal. Aside from his wife and five children—my mother was fourth in the pecking order—relatives and friends were also inevitably around the enormous ebony dining room table, lured by my grandmother Ida's legendary hospitality.

Aunt Marcy was particularly close to her father; even in the presence of her siblings she never referred to him as "our father" but as "my father." Throughout her long life, all she had to do was tell one story centered on this Friday night ritual to assert herself as Willy's girl:

"Pop's oldest friend, Max, calls him on a Monday morning. What he had to say could not be discussed on the phone, so he insisted that they meet at Lou Siegel's restaurant for lunch.

"'Willy, I'm shocked,' Max barked, his face inches away from his bewildered lunch companion's. 'I knew you even before you married Ida, and now there are five children. Don't you dare lie to me!'

"My father only stared back in silence.

"'I saw the big blonde pull up in that Packard of yours in front of the Turkish bath and wait for you to come out, and you went off with her! Don't you dare lie to me!' Max repeated.

"My father howled with laughter, saying, 'It was Marcy, my second oldest!'"

Forever empowered by her father's sponsorship, Aunt Marcy basked in the pleasure of their unique relationship and delighted in her pride of place, and at ninety she was still telling her story. Freud would have had a picnic.

FATHER PETER

Simon and Werner's was on East 110th Street, between First and Second Avenues in Harlem, next to St. Ann's Church. The business, built by my grandfather, had remained vital in this perpetually decaying neighborhood, which had seen ethnic tides over the decades. When Willy Simon's own children were young, East Harlem was a rough Italian enclave surrounding the market. The locals shopped here too, accommodated by my grandfather, who omitted for them the costly rules of *kashruth* attending the slaughter of poultry meant for the Jews.

Peter Rofrano was a bag boy in the market who wrapped the freshly killed poultry. A neighborhood waif, he had endeared himself to my grandfather, who gradually absorbed the urchin into his own family. Close in age to my mother and her younger brother Jerry, Peter was soon part of a lively Jewish tribe living uptown. While the warmth of the Simons was lavished on Peter, my grandfather knew that it was no substitute for the boy's own traditions. In that spirit, Willy Simon saw to Peter's Catholic education.

Insulated from the harsh realities of the East Harlem neighborhood by my grandfather's patronage, Peter thrived in the local parochial school. For a street kid, an academic path was a rarity, yet his progress grew less surprising the more embedded he became within my family. His decision as a teenager to become a priest, though, took everyone by surprise, but it also made the Simons very proud.

When the time came for Peter to pursue his calling, my grandfather sent him off to Rome. He was delighted to be Peter's unlikely spiritual steward, the brand of his religion of little import to him. After all, neither of his own sons had been tempted much by Judaism, let alone a career as a clergyman. Following Peter's return to New York, my grandfather put his diplomatic skills to work on the local Catholic establishment, helping to ensure Peter's appointment as a priest at St. Ann's.

So unusual was it for a local to make good and find his way back to the neighborhood as a priest that a parade was organized to accompany Peter from his temporary accommodations in midtown to St. Ann's. There the young priest was greeted by a band, along with clerics, politicians, and none other than Francis Cardinal Spellman.

Peter emerged from the lead car of the cavalcade and went directly to the entry of the chicken market, where my grandfather, dressed not in his customary overalls but a suit, was respectfully awaiting him. Peter would have none of his mentor's formality and threw his arms around the man who had made such a difference in his life. Willy actually had to remind the tearful Peter about the waiting cardinal, sending the young priest on his way—forever gone but always next door.

As a child, whenever I visited the market I called in at St. Ann's as well. Inside the grand doors there was a wide, steep staircase, and at its top stood women in long, crisp skirts and white origami-like hats that hid their hair and pulled back their cheeks. The only sound I remember was the rustling of their garments as they ushered me into a dark wooden room. There stood Father Peter, whose smile welcomed me. Sensing my discomfort in the presence of the nuns, he would kneel to my level, putting me at ease.

"There's a reason why G-d made those ladies look so funny, Petey Boy. Because I'm such a handful to look after, they need to be a bit scary. After all, if they looked like your ma or Aunt Marcy I just wouldn't behave myself," he'd say. Variations on our playful routine occurred for many years, long after the nuns had been demythologized by the reforms of Vatican II.

I did not see Peter again until my mother died decades later and I came home from China for her funeral. He sat with the mourners in the front pew, his stiff white collar making perfect sense amongst the tearful Jews.

Once back in Beijing following the *shiva*, I was greeted by a distinguished gentleman who showed up at my office for a chat about the lay of the land. His business card radiated conflicting signals: a flowery Italian name alongside the logo of a lily-white California-based engineering firm. Before working our way through the usual topics—a lack of housing for foreigners, no cash machines, taxi shortages—I discovered that my guest was, in fact, from East 111th Street in Harlem. Not only had he known my grandfather, but he had worked at Simon and Werner's after school, bagging the freshly killed poultry to be loaded onto the company's delivery truck, and Father Peter had given him his first Communion.

Here I was in the middle of Beijing, as far away from my grandfather and Father Peter as I could be. The only thing more thrilling than being joined to them in foreign parts by this stranger was my growing awareness of such rare constellations as magically pedestrian.

THE GARDENIA BUSH

Amongst my earliest memories is that of planting a gardenia bush in the bare front garden of Michael-Ann's new house on Bayshore Drive in Miami Beach. Her parents, the Russells, had been newlyweds along with mine in Miami during the early 1950s. While my father got involved in the building boom of hotels on The Beach—I remember seeing, Amarcord-like, the hoisting of an enormous brown crystal chandelier in the lobby of the Eden Roc hotel—Bob Russell struck it rich in the scrap-metal business at the time of the Korean War. The Russells then moved to a new home, with a white baby grand piano on a stone platform in the middle of the living room.

Though Michael-Ann was a few years my senior, we were thrown together because our parents were close. As a little boy, I took riding lessons where she did, but refused to continue after being forced to stretch out, terrified, along a horse's spine. I had dancing lessons, too, which ended after I somehow knocked over a huge plant during a little girl's routine. Michael-Ann and I both loved the water, and I tagged along with her to the hotel pool, even after being duped by a lifeguard into jumping off the high board wearing a tube whose valve had been deliberately opened.

Our mothers could have been sisters, both stylish blondes,

though separated by a foot in height. They were both in disastrous marriages as well, though Muriel Russell persevered through frequent separations. She became a philanthropist whose good works enabled her to inhabit a world parallel to her husband's long after my own parents had divorced. And at the time of the divorce, as my mother, Aunt Marcy, and I— with Marlowe, my stuffed poodle in my arms—pulled away from our house in Coral Gables for the very last time, bound for New York, there was Muriel, sweeping off the front steps in preparation for the people who were about to move in. But we did not lose touch. When Muriel made frequent trips to New York to see her own mother, Nana, she always carved out time for a visit with us.

Years passed, with more episodic separations between Muriel and Bob; news of Michael-Ann's marriage and the birth of her son; finally Michael-Ann's divorce and subsequent remarriage. Then one night, as I called my mother from the phone booth in the basement of my Princeton dorm, my blasé check-in was derailed by her sobs while she told how Michael-Ann, her son Jonathan, and their nanny had been amongst the passengers on board a plane that had crashed in the Everglades. What first sprang to my mind was a newspaper photo of Michael-Ann as a little girl being greeted by her mother, arms outstretched, after the young camper had been rescued from a flood during a summer sojourn in Pennsylvania. On the night of the Everglades tragedy, Bob, overcome by the news, suffered a heart attack in the Miami Airport.

My mother, again in regular touch with old friends and even with my father, finally spoke to Muriel herself once she was able to take calls. Muriel's loss so outweighed anything my mother was experiencing as a struggling single parent that her own dramas seemed to be forgotten. Nana, in Florida caring for Muriel, pronounced my mother's calls comforting and encouraged the two friends to speak often.

Over time even such horror made room for different kinds of news. Bob recovered from his heart attack, took up tennis, and began living with a younger woman. Muriel threw herself into a project, endowing a center of education connected to her local synagogue in memory of Michael-Ann and Jonathan, and also had a man named Herb in her life.

During my first trip to Florida after the accident, I called Muriel, who promptly invited me to visit her grand penthouse on the water. The normality of her welcome was disarming— a warm hug accompanied by questions about school, plans, and the future. She took my hand, and we walked into the cavernous living room—the white piano was by the window— where Herb awaited us. Like a schoolgirl with a crush, she introduced us. After Muriel settled herself, I looked into her eyes for some clue about what to do next. It is only now that I can describe Muriel's expression: a mask fixed with Botox in days long before it had been invented. Muriel sat very close to Herb on the sofa, clearly needing to be in physical contact with this lovely gentleman. I felt they were trying to put me at ease as I babbled on about everything but those who were no longer with us. Surrounded by walls and tabletops filled with memorabilia, I caught sight of a photo of Michael-Ann on a horse as a little girl and began speaking of her. Suddenly, Muriel's mask gave way to a smile.

—

To those who had long known the Russells, news of their impending divorce five years later was greeted with skepticism. After all, it had been mooted so often through the years. But Muriel alerted my mother to her arrival in New York, volunteering details of the legal procedure about to take place in the city. They arranged to meet up immediately after the deed was done. There, on 57th Street, my mother awaited Muriel at the Russian Tea Room. The appointed hour came and went, my mother long nursing a drink. She finally gave up and walked home to her nearby apartment, where she rang Muriel's hotel and left messages. Hours later Muriel called, sounding dazed, and reported that en route to the lawyer's office to sign the papers Bob had died in the taxi and she was now his widow.

It was a long time before I next saw Muriel as teaching at various schools around America and a posting abroad had conspired against a reunion. Then, during my Beijing stint for Manufacturers Hanover Trust Company in the early 1980s, I received a telex from Muriel saying that she and Herb would be visiting China. I offered to help with their plans, assuring them that they would be well looked after.

Closer to their arrival, they invited me to the newly opened Maxim's. On the appointed evening, I got to the restaurant and was swiftly shown to a table where Muriel and Herb awaited me, sitting side by side in a banquette. When I requested a menu in Chinese, they became positively giddy, their bubbly attention making me briefly forget just how uncomfortable I was to be with Muriel, on whose losses I remained fixated. As we ate supper, I noticed a sylph of a woman walking near my chair, her image caught in the mirror hanging on the wall behind my dinner partners. As she wafted by, the scent of gardenias drifted in the slipstream of her chiffon stole.

"By any chance, Muriel, do you remember the gardenia bush Michael-Ann and I planted when you moved into your new house?" I asked. A smile enveloped her face, and she leaned toward me.

We then spent the rest of the evening happily chatting about her daughter, who was now very much with us. When we parted, Muriel thanked me, saying, "It helps me to know that I wasn't dreaming."

CUTTING AGAINST THE GRAIN

After my parents' divorce when I was eight, we were in limbo. Our house in Coral Gables, Florida, had been sold, and we were about to move to New York. My mother's elder cousin Nat and his wife Bess, Palm Beach grandees, invited us for a farewell supper. Although my mother was happy to drive, they insisted on sending their car and chauffeur for us, which I thought was neat. I became happily lost in the backseat, cosseted in fragrant leather, identifying the makes of other cars as we motored northward.

When we arrived, having swept up a curving drive to the house, its doors swung open and we were greeted so effusively I could not help but think the welcome was meant for others. Some unknown relatives awaited us inside the unrelentingly elegant house, which seemed to shrink its guests into insignificance. I didn't know how to sit right in my chair, its peculiar proportions and padding thwarting my ease. I was adrift not only amongst strangers but in the conversation as well; names were mentioned, only to be swiftly replaced by others. Thus I was relieved when a man in a black suit silently appeared in the sitting room and announced supper.

Bess made a big deal about my sitting to her right, where again I found myself in a chair that didn't work. A lady in a costume, which I later learned was a maid's uniform, suddenly placed a tomato-shaped glass bowl in front of me. Though eager to eat the red soup, I was daunted by the array of cutlery spread out on either side of the bowl. Fortunately, my mother caught my eye and made a minor show of selecting the right spoon, which was too big.

Beneath the table, I noticed Bess's foot resting on a treadle, moving it up and down from time to time. It eventually dawned on me that people appeared soon after she touched it. Without missing a spoonful, I stepped on the treadle to test my theory. It was correct. The man in the black suit soon hovered beside Bess, awaiting word from her. None was forthcoming—not even a glance in his direction. I smiled at him; he left; and shortly thereafter I did it again. When the scene was repeated, I decided it was no fun making that man come out only to be ignored by a lady I hardly knew and already didn't like.

The glass bowls were shortly removed, and a massive tray was then held stiffly at my side. I was paralyzed by the mysterious choices offered, and my mother immediately came to the rescue, telling the gentleman the kind of meat I liked, even requesting the end piece and crispy potatoes. At least when the vegetables came I could recognize string beans.

I was hungry, and the food looked really good, even though it appeared oddly miniature, dwarfed by my enormous plate. I now knew to watch my mother for cues in selecting an appropriate fork and knife. The size of the silverware, however, made it difficult to cut up my portion of meat, and even more difficult to keep my battle a secret with all that clacking of silver against china. I suddenly felt Bess's spidery hand on my left sleeve. I downed tools, and my eyes locked on hers.

"You might be cutting against the grain, my dear," she suggested.

In an attempt to ignore her alien words, I looked around the big table, feeling like a piece of meat myself in the middle of a plate that was too big. Then I unlaced the brown oxford on my left foot, stood up, placed it in the center of the table's immaculate cloth, and sat down, feeling comfortable for the very first time that evening. Someone kicked me. It wasn't my mother because she was too far away. I then rose again, retrieved my shoe, sat down, and ate all my beans and potatoes. Time unfroze above the table, with conversation quickening amongst the guests about everything but my shoe and me.

Finally back in the big car, my mother held me close, telling me that she understood perfectly why I had put my shoe on the table. "Be that as it may, Cookie, do try another way of expressing yourself when people are being silly," she chided.

After we moved to New York and were established in a new apartment, a large box arrived, a house-warming gift from Nat and Bess. We gingerly unwrapped the exquisite package to discover a hideous crystal vase. Unable to bring herself to feign approval and gratitude, my mother just threw her head back, laughed, and put the vase back in its box. In a few months she got word that Bess was coming to New York and wanted to drop in. Immediately before her arrival my mother retrieved the vase and placed it prominently on a shelf in the foyer. When Bess arrived, she made a big fuss about the apartment and was keen to hear all about life in New York. As we chatted, she casually wandered around the apartment, commenting on various decorating highlights.

While she was out of our sight on her walkabout, we heard her exclaim, "What a stunning vase, Harriet! Where did you get it?"

"You'll never guess, dear. You gave it to us as a house-warming gift," my mother replied. Bess then confessed her embarrassment at singling out her present—of all things.

After Bess departed, my mother took my hand, walked toward the dining room, removed a high-heeled shoe, and put it right in the center of the table.

GUSSIE'S EYES

At family gatherings, we sometimes watched movies of my mother's elder sisters' weddings. Aunt Birdie had been married in the early 1920s at a hotel on Fifth Avenue and 59th Street, a site now occupied by the General Motors Building. The film of this occasion dwells endlessly on the receiving line, with guests ascending a very grand staircase. Of greatest interest to me was the footage of groomsmen using walking sticks to make a tunnel through which the newlyweds strolled and shots of my mother as a little girl scampering amongst the guests.

But the movie of Aunt Marcy's wedding a couple of years later provides a richer historical record of my family and the times. The latest technology had liberated the camera from the tripod, so rather than remaining focused on a staircase, it was able to record more animated footage. Doves are released at the end of the ceremony, and my paternal grandparents—neither of whom I had known—are seen nuzzling each other. My mother's younger brother, a bewigged page boy at Birdie's wedding, pretends to smoke a cigarette behind the back of his charismatic father. Then there comes an infamous quartet: two couples together at one table, both of whom were later divorced, with the ex-husband of one pair marrying the ex-wife of the other. There are also scenes of Gussie, my mother's eldest first cousin by decades, doing the Charleston with great abandon in the silence of those days before talkies, but with such power that the dance seems to supply its own music. This was my introduction to Gussie.

The man Gussie had married, Sam Schiff, became a significant player in the New Deal. He owned a company that provided Robert Moses with the cement used to build the roads and bridges throughout New York. Sam was commercially related to James Farley, President Roosevelt's postmaster general. But despite Sam's social and political ascent Gussie took on no airs, continuing to serve her famous chicken-in-the-pot to Jim Farley and his pals when they came to supper at her Manhattan Beach mansion.

Three decades later Aunt Birdie was diagnosed with terminal cancer, and her sickroom became the family's center of gravity. Our clan—I was nine at the time—would gather for Friday night supper in the dining room of her Grand Concourse apartment, with various relatives showing up for either the meal or dessert. Gussie would appear for the latter, her drive too long for an earlier arrival. She owned an enormous Cadillac, which she commanded rather than drove, and she wore a diamond ring worthy of a kiss. Such luxuries aside, Gussie seemed to be a Jewish version of Tugboat Annie, appearing to pay no mind to her clothes, though it was invariably mentioned by others that she only bought the best.

Gussie would park herself on the sunken sofa with a huge tote bag at her side. Although I didn't understand much of the conversation during those evenings—it always seemed to be about unknown relatives—I loved the way her eyes virtually disappeared when she smiled. Gussie would survey the room, asking someone she had not met before, "Wanna hat?" followed by "What color?" Then at the end of the evening, she would reach into her bag and produce a crocheted beret in the color of choice. To me, she was a magician.

Later I again found myself in her company at a new cousin's bris, the Jewish rite of circumcision. She was holding court in the den, where those too squeamish to witness the ceremony had taken refuge. She did no crocheting on that hot June day but worked the room, talking to children and adults in exactly the same fashion. I watched carefully how she honed in on a new acquaintance with playful intensity, her face mirroring the age of the person at whom she gazed.

The next day, though, Gussie suffered a massive stroke, which doomed her to years of paralysis and dependence. I occasionally visited her in her daughter's garden, where she sat limply strapped into a wheelchair, no longer in charge. Though her eyes gaped, finally affording me the opportunity to see them, they were now opaque. Only when they had been hidden by the smile that took over her face did they give me her measure.

Gussie was eventually sent to a residential home on the eastern end of Long Island. On a regular basis, Aunt Marcy visited Gussie and brought her pastrami sandwiches, knowing that the WASPy fare of the institution was unbearable to

Gussie—hardly the chicken-in-the-pot served up to Jim Farley a lifetime before.

As the years wore on, old age compounded Gussie's infirmities. Near the end of her life, I went to visit her. Aunt Marcy held her elder cousin's hand, the pastrami sandwich left uneaten on a nearby table.

On our way out, we stopped for a quick chat with the nurses as one piped up, "Can you imagine? Mrs. Schiff keeps rambling about visiting the White House and attending President Roosevelt's inaugurations."

Aunt Marcy sighed and informed the nurse, "It's true."

Turning to leave, she could at least feel assured that Gussie would be held in esteem, if only briefly. And as I departed, rhythmic Charleston music roared back and broke the sad silence of farewell.

THE "FLORIDA ONE"

As a young child in the 1950s, I belonged to a Coral Gables Cub Scout troop. When I was seven, it was announced at a meeting that we would be guests on a kiddy show featuring The Little Rascals, known also as the Our Gang comedies. These black-and-white films were peopled with a diverse band, including Spanky, the caring ringleader; Alfalfa, the temperamental divo with his signature cowlick; Buckwheat, the irresistible caricature of a little black kid; and Darla, the upwardly mobile Miss Perfect. There were also Tubby, Weezer, and Pee Wee the dog, with a black circle around one eye.

On the appointed day, we were ferried to the studio in a station wagon. Next to me was Neil Grossman, a short guy from the neighborhood, and on the way to the studio he told me the funniest joke I had ever heard.

Upon arrival, the troop crowded into the studio, and, as usual, I was banished to the back row because I was tall for my age. The broadcast would be live, so we were prepped. During the natural breaks in the episodes, the host would be chatting with us.

I felt disoriented. At home I would watch the show seated in front of our blond wood DuMont television. It had doors, so when scary things suddenly appeared—like Gabby Hays blowing Puffed Wheat out of a cannon or coming attractions for The Creature from the Black Lagoon—I could jump behind those doors to shield myself from terror. At home I knew my place: watching in front of the set. But in the studio I was somehow inside the television while still watching myself, Spanky, and friends on the monitors.

During the first break from the film, the emcee worked the front row. But rather than making small talk with my troopmates, he put each on the spot by asking for a joke. After several "knock-knock" and shaggy dog ordeals, he came to Neil, whom I had expected to steal the show by telling the very joke I had heard in the back of the station wagon, but such was not the case. Though perplexed by his choice, I couldn't believe my good fortune at possibly being able to tell that joke myself.

After more intervals, the emcee stood in front of me with the mic shoved in my face, and requested a joke.

"Why did the little boy put his head down the toilet?" I asked, beaming. So excited was I at the chance to tell the joke that even before the emcee could ask why—if he had ever intended to—I answered, "Because he wanted to say, 'Howdy Doody.'"

I knew my friends loved the joke, judging by the wave of laughter, but I also knew something was wrong. Not a word of approval came from the emcee as he snatched the mic away. There was sudden movement around us, and the monitors again showed the comedy, with no introduction by the emcee. We were then asked to leave the set. My mother was standing in the wings, amongst other grown-ups, puffing on a cigarette. When she caught sight of me, she exhaled, sighed deeply, and came toward me. Fresh from my triumphant performance, I was expecting her to congratulate me on a joke well told. Instead, she just looked at me, apparently conflicted by pride felt for a cute son who told a naughty joke on live TV and embarrassment for the very same reason. After her initial paralysis, she engulfed me in a very warm hug, which felt more protective than affectionate.

On the raucous drive home, my friends, save Neil, asked me to repeat the joke several times.

When I opened our front door, Odessa, our housekeeper, enfolded me in her fleshy arms and drawled, "Why did you have to tell that one, Sugar?"

Several days later a typewritten letter arrived for me from Mr. Sam Ferry, the man who headed up the Scouts in Florida. My parents read it to me, explaining its contents. He said that I had disgraced the Cub Scouts in public when I told my joke on television, and he dismissed me from the troop.

My parents could not bring themselves to be stern, sensing my genuine confusion. They delivered a halfhearted lecture on matters of judgment, making the point that my friends' delight did not mean I had done the right thing. Their tone softened yet further when explaining that Wednesday afternoons would no longer be spent in my Cub Scout den. Under her breath, my mother muttered something about the folly of a childless man being the head of the Cub Scouts.

My parents soon went their separate ways, my father staying in Florida while my mother and I moved to New York. Some months later, in the midst of my awkward adjustment in New York, my mother suggested that I might benefit from rejoining the Cub Scouts. She had done her homework, and we were off one evening to P.S. 90, where I was warmly welcomed by the troop and troopmaster. I filled out all the forms but declined a pamphlet about a shop that provided regulation uniforms. After all, I still had mine, though the trouser cuffs would probably have to be let down a bit.

A postcard soon arrived announcing the next meeting. Off I went again, where I fully participated in events and joined in the recitation of the Scout pledge, the words of which were akin to those of the national anthem—known, repeated, and not really taken on board. After all, what does "to be square" really mean?

Then the troupmaster steered me over to a corner of the room, asking, "Peter, may I have a quiet word with you?"

As he went on to welcome me into the troop, give me details of activities, and offer encouraging words, my spirits lifted. But then, as I made my way back to the others, he whispered, "We know about you."

HARVEY'S DIGITS

Aunt Marcy and Uncle Dave's two sons, Harvey and Joel, were both born with six toes on each foot. On Friday nights in New York, when our extended family always gathered, sometimes the topic would come up at the supper table. What began as a jovial comment about genetics often deteriorated into a one-sided argument, with Uncle Dave adamantly proclaiming that no such deformity could ever have come from his side of the family, which made everyone else more convinced that it could only have come from his genes.

These cousins, who were ten and twenty years my senior, became the nearest thing I had to brothers. Joel, the younger of the two, had a mane of blond hair, extraordinary blue eyes, a low threshold for embarrassment, and a social awkwardness that certainly didn't hamper his success with the girls; Joel was the apple of his father's eye, as well as being adored by my mother, who often remarked that they were kindred Geminis. For Aunt Marcy, though, there was only Harvey. In early childhood photos, he looked terribly appealing—playful and dapper. As Marcy's son, it was no surprise that he was Willy Simon's favorite grandson. My mother once quipped that it was because Harvey liked to eat scallions as a little boy, just like our patriarch did, that assured Harvey of his honored position.

Harvey would periodically stay with us in Florida after he got his first job as a salesman for Walt Disney, even before there was a Disney World. He once took me deep-sea fishing without telling my parents, and when we finally got home after that long day he caught hell from my mother, with my fish barely noticed in the fray. He always seemed to be showing up with towels he had stolen from hotels on his beat, leaving my mother puzzled and annoyed, since we had enough of our own towels and she genuinely disapproved of such behavior.

Even so, Harvey and I became closer following my move to New York. There, his toes established some street cred for me. After lunch one day in the schoolyard, I overheard a discussion amongst a bunch of students trying to outdo one another by describing weird family members. Suddenly it dawned on me that I just might be able to one-up everyone and thus get their attention and admiration.

"Both my cousins have six toes on each foot!" I blurted out.

Nobody believed me, but rather than simply desisting I called Harvey, asking him for proof.

"Kids in school called me a liar because they didn't believe that you and Joel have six toes on each foot," I explained.

"No one is going to call my favorite cousin a liar! Either you can beat them up or I can send you a picture," he offered, knowing full well the option I would choose.

When Harvey's photo arrived in the mail, I proudly

shoved it in the faces of as many kids I dared approach, their eyes out on stalks after taking a good look.

Those twelve toes gave me air cover, helping me settle into New York without a father and into the schoolyard without athletic prowess.

ETHEL MERMAN WAS PRETTY GOOD

Soon after moving to New York City, I planned to go to camp for the summer with three neighbors from our building—Stevie, Andy, and Albert. I was pleased to be going away with these new friends because it made me feel that I was beginning to belong. We called ourselves the "Black Hawks."

Already the Black Hawks had saved me from being embarrassed because of my lack of athletic ability. In Florida, my shortcomings had not been obvious because I had been used to flying kites, riding bicycles, and swimming, but such activities were hardly on offer in my New York City school, where in no time I was being picked last for punchball games. However, the Black Hawks soon helped me get the hang of stickball in the long alley between our building and the next. Also, while Stevie and Andy's parents were a tight foursome, Albert and I were being raised by our mothers. His father, a professional musician, had died very young. His mother Matilda, tiny and severely crippled with polio yet a writer of children's books and an employee at her brother's accounting firm, had hit it off with my mother.

Since vaccines were required for camp, I went to see Dr. Tacktill, a jolly bald man with a significant underbite. He had warned me that there might be a mild reaction to the cocktail of booster inoculations. In fact, the shots triggered a series of fierce ear infections so the Black Hawks left without me. When I finally got to camp, rather than alighting with a crowd already sharing an adventure on a bus, I stepped meekly from my father's Buick into a deserted driveway leading to a clapboard office.

While my father, who happened to be in New York, was keen to settle me in at camp as swiftly as possible and be gone, my mother was intent on repeatedly making it clear to the staff that swimming was strictly prohibited by my doctor; furthermore, if eventually I was allowed to plunge in, I was to first stuff my ears with lamb's wool and put on a bathing cap. At that moment, I vowed that my ears would remain a problem all summer because there was no way I was going to wear a bathing cap in the lake.

At camp I felt disadvantaged not only athletically but socially, since I had gotten it in my head that the alliances formed on the bus to camp and in the early days—occasions I had missed—seemed impenetrable. Worse, the Black Hawks had been split up, and although Albert and I were still together, Stevie and Andy were bunking elsewhere. Not only did I not have support from the Black Hawks out on the playing fields, but my bunkmates had made it clear that the only activity worse than arts and crafts was drama.

Surprisingly, Don the drama counselor, with his pasty complexion, loud Southern accent, and arms constantly in motion, was certainly different from the others looking after us. When we were taken to the rec hall for his sessions, there was no small talk between Don and the other counselors, who seemed to escape rather than depart. One day Don announced that we would be staging the musical *Gypsy* for the second parents' weekend. At the prospect of having to sing and dance in public, I groaned along with the others, but secretly I looked forward to participating.

Surprisingly, Don assigned me to play Herbie, the father of June and Louise. All at once I was thrilled by the recognition, ill at ease at being publicly identified with drama, and terrified at the prospect of performing. Quickly, though, I became involved in the show that was to rescue me from the playing fields. Gradually, my athletic awkwardness was being dwarfed by the fact that I was needed elsewhere.

Although I was unfamiliar with this show's tunes, music had always been around me. We had a hi-fi at home, and it was on a lot; I took piano lessons; and my mother liked to sing and play the piano. I had also been taken to various musical events, from Broadway shows to classical concerts and dance performances.

As the summer wore on and the show began to take shape, the campers gave me a wider berth, their deference suggesting that I was becoming special. Visiting day soon came, and it was show time. Something happened to me that Saturday evening. The exhilaration of gliding across the stage to "Some People" seemed the same as that of hitting a home run. For me, the joyously rowdy reception of the audience was a transformative thrill.

Back in the city at summer's end, my mother announced that the next Saturday we would be going to see a Broadway matinee, along with Albert. We went to see *Gypsy,* but I was confused; while it had the same name and storyline as the show we had performed at camp, my part as Herbie the father had become that of a mother named Rose. I sang along but fell quiet when lots of naked ladies appeared on the stage, with one playing a trumpet and another lighting up like a Christmas tree. When the ovation finally died down and the house lights came on, I poked Albert in the ribs and said that even though the naked ladies stole the show, the woman who played my part—someone named Ethel Merman—was pretty good.

Years later I saw Ethel Merman, whom Cole Porter likened to a brass band, working as a volunteer in the gift shop of Roosevelt Hospital. There was no way she could have suspected the bond between us.

BEAR MOUNTAIN RECORDER

One year on a day trip away from summer camp we traveled to Bear Mountain, south of West Point on the Hudson River. Just setting off was fun. The bus passed through an easement on the grounds of Camp NYDA, which stood for New York Diabetic Association. As we made our way, we burst out singing "Sugar in the morning, sugar in the evening, sugar at suppertime..." Predictably, dozens of diabetics flipped us the bird.

While at Bear Mountain, I bought a souvenir recorder, the kind of flute I had learned to play in school. My new one, though, was red and shiny, with the state park's logo wrapped around it just below the mouthpiece. After I'd practiced a bit, my party piece was to play it up my nose; once back in the city I regaled friends as my clownish repertoire grew.

One morning I noticed a mark where my nostril met my face but thought little of it. After all, in those pre-adolescent days, a blemish was no tragedy. Who cared what girls thought, anyway? But gradually the mark began to spread, reaching into my nostril. I remained determined to make the rash disappear, resorting to lots of soap to address the problem. Finally defeated, I was forced to bring the matter to my mother's attention.

Off to Dr. Tacktill we went. After a long wait in his office, my mother and I were ushered into his examination room. When I pointed at my nose, he instantly pronounced the problem impetigo and gave me some salve to be applied regularly to the strep-induced rash.

When we were almost out the door, he called to my mother and asked, "By the way, Harriet, does he ever put anything up his nose?"

Her ensuing silence, long by any standard, seemed all the more so because of the humiliation awaiting me if she told him about the recorder.

"No," she slowly replied, and we left.

Once out in the street, despite my gratitude for her perjury on my behalf I knew that the silence of our stroll home was best left undisturbed. Finally, we passed through the front gate of our building and continued through the hushed and huge art deco lobby, with the clack of my mother's heels echoing along the way. She led me into our apartment—number 112. Moving with balletic grace, she entered my room, opened the bureau drawer, removed my red recorder, snapped it across her thigh, and dropped the pieces into the wastepaper basket. Then, with genuine concern, she urged me to begin applications of the salve immediately.

THE WITNESS

P.S. 90, which was at the corner of Sheridan and McClellan Streets, was an unusual school, with students who were blind or retarded (the term used at the time) occupying the two lower floors, leaving the upper two floors to the rest of us. Though there was little contact between these diverse groups, the mix did leave a lasting impression.

One day en route to class on the fourth floor of P.S. 90 with my friends, we decided to check out one of the bathrooms on a floor reserved for the special students, a part of the school we'd rarely had the opportunity to visit. While tentatively opening the door, we caught sight of some boys vandalizing the walls of the toilet. Upon spotting us, they swept us aside and tore out of there, disappearing down the institutional green hallway. That we didn't recognize any of the culprits served us well, allowing us to present ourselves as witnesses to an incident. We were, nonetheless, conflicted, since by coming forward we knew we would be obliged to explain our presence on the floor.

Ultimately we took the view that civic duty far outweighed the perils of explaining our whereabouts—and we'd gotten it right. Once we reached class, Mrs. Kraf, the wife of our state senator, with her terrifying butch haircut and whiskey voice, focused only on our ability to recount what had happened. She immediately dispatched someone to fetch Dr. Di Napoli, the principal, whose very presence would bring us to our feet as a gesture of respect. He was a lovely gentleman, with steel-gray, wavy hair and always dressed in a three-piece suit.

As we settled back in chairs at our double desks, with their disused inkwells and seasoned stains, Dr. Di Napoli confessed how disturbed he was that the school's most vulnerable students had been exposed to danger by a group of errant thugs. He asked the witnesses to rise, commending us on our willingness to come forward and slyly mentioning our fortuitous presence on the lower floor. Then he turned straight to me and asked me to recount what I had seen.

"We were just entering the toilet on the second floor when we saw these kids *schmearing* goo on the walls," I faithfully reported, by which time both principal and teacher were stifling laughter.

Baffled by their shared mirth—this didn't happen to witnesses on *Perry Mason*—I longed for a trapdoor through which I could drop and be rescued from public humiliation.

Dr. Di Napoli finally spoke, expressing gratitude for the narrative then adding, "How about picking your vocabulary a bit more carefully."

After dutifully rewinding the account in my head, I began again: "We were just entering the lavatory on the second floor…"

Once more they laughed, prompting me to start yet again.

I then went on to change *goo* to *toothpaste,* leaving *schmear* unaltered.

Puzzled by their continued merriment, I was nonetheless put at ease when he said my words had been much appreciated, though the fact that I had not recognized the offenders was unfortunate. There would be no reason for further inquiry, he commented as he and Mrs. Kraf left the classroom. After hearing guffaws from the hall, Mrs. Kraf reentered, finally composing herself by the time she reached her desk.

That evening at supper, after I recounted the details of my testimony and my mother had calmed herself following her own fits of laughter, she explained that there was no such word as *schmear* in English.

"Maybe you've been spending too much time with Aunt Marcy," she quipped, crediting her sister with my word choice.

I didn't get it, and my face must have registered panic at the prospect of my time with Aunt Marcy being jeopardized over a matter of vocabulary.

"I'm just kidding, Cookie," she quietly added, calming me with a touch on the cheek.

A SHARED WOUND

*B*y the sixth grade, I had stopped lying about my father. No longer did I tell friends that he was away on a business trip or working late. The corrosion of his absence, though, continued despite my ability to tell the truth.

One day Mrs. Kraf, with whom I enjoyed the privilege of participating in the Individualized Reading Program, which allowed me to zoom through books and chat with her about them, asked us to write a composition about someone in our class whom we admired. I chose Jeff, a dashing and affable athlete. He lived in a walk-up building on the other side of the Grand Concourse from me. My essay, which focused on Jeff's athletic prowess and good cheer, included a comment about my envy of anyone whose parents were not divorced.

A few days later Mrs. Kraf took me aside, first offering assurance that there was nothing to worry about. She asked that I stop by after school for a chat, her voice oddly warm as she made her request. I arrived punctually but still uneasy about the summons. When I entered the office, there sat Jeff. Beckoning me to sit beside him, Mrs. Kraf drew up a chair, facing us both. Holding some papers in her hands, she told us of something extraordinary: we had each chosen the other to admire, and both of us had divorced parents!

That Jeff said he admired me seemed inconceivable;

beyond that, I was comforted by the coincidence, which was never again discussed. Disarmed by the realization that he could still seem perfect to me, I was helped to see myself as someone more than merely a fatherless child.

BETWEEN THE ACTS

$\mathcal{M}$y mother was regarded as a miracle, conceived after my grandmother had been told there would be no more children. A pouting blonde with a heart murmur, she was incandescently bright and grew to be a stunning woman, likened to Lauren Bacall and Simone Signoret, but she never believed she was pretty. The failure of her late marriage only weakened her confidence. Although I had assumed that her vulnerability was a natural product of her divorce, I gleaned from family stories that it was a specific incident in her youth that had triggered her emotional fragility. Her own mother had been seriously ill, and the rest of the family had gone out to an event, leaving my mother at home with her. My mother had gone to bed, and her mother had called out. In a stupor, my mother stumbled out of bed, somehow hitting her head so seriously that she was knocked unconscious. In the morning, she had a streak of white hair at each temple and was forever changed.

Eventually, ground down by divorce, her sister Birdie's death, return to full-time employment, and my father's remarriage, my mother suffered a nervous breakdown. She looked like a stranger when I caught sight of her as I bounded off the bus from camp one summer. Soon she was hospitalized at Hillside in Glen Oaks on Long Island, entering under the condition that she be allowed to attend my bar mitzvah in late December.

At dawn on that day, she was spirited out of the hospital so I could walk to Temple Adath Israel with her from our apartment building on the Grand Concourse rather than from Aunt Marcy's a few blocks away, where I was living. The charade had to be maintained because of my mother's lurking suspicion that, owing to her illness, my father would seek custody of me. Little chance of that! He had already abandoned his new wife and disappeared. I was uncertain whether he would even show up. Yet when my paternal grandmother entered the synagogue and took a seat next to my radiant mother, sitting across the aisle from her was her long-absent son. There is little I remember of that day: an itchy wool suit, my mother quietly leaving our home at dusk to return to the hospital, my father simply gone again.

After her hospitalization—the first of several—my mother was keen to get beyond her troubled period, displaying heartfelt enthusiasm for brightened days. With everyone's attention so focused on her renascence, there was no appreciation of the damage that had been done to me during her ordeal. As I was always regarded by doctors and relatives as critical to her well-being, the assumption was that if she were healthy I would be, too. I was always hovering, arms outstretched, though never able to cushion her inevitable fall.

She was soon stepping back into her life, and, at about

this time, we started to bump into Stelly, her first cousin, and Stelly's son David at various family functions. Although Stelly was considerably younger than my mother, her son was just one year my junior. That she, too, was divorced created a bond between the two women that drew us all together in a way that blood had not. We lived close to each other, with visits becoming frequent and David and I happily developing a friendship separate from our mothers'.

My mother went to work at City Center, bringing her closer to the cultural life of New York, which she had always enjoyed, and it was my good fortune to tag along. Once, in search of a bathroom at a City Center Christmas party, I made a wrong turn and found myself on stage, where Baryshnikov was rehearsing. He kindly showed me the way. On other occasions, I had lunch with my mother and Judith Jamison and Beverly Sills at the luncheonette opposite the theater's loading dock. I was learning to take on her breeziness about New York's gifts without ever growing complacent.

Gradually, Stelly and David got caught up in my mother's brand of New York life, and what Stelly brought to the table was a social vitality that managed to trump my mother's reticence. The two women began going to events together on Saturday evenings and Sunday afternoons. Soon my cerebral mother's departure from her books—she would speak of them almost as friends—got my attention rather than the details of her destinations. David and I started hearing about Parents Without Partners (PWP), an organization that not only catered to our mothers but had activities that included us as well.

One day we were told that PWP was hosting a deep-sea fishing expedition, and we would all be going along. There was much preparation leading up to the excursion. Aunt Marcy, delighted by her sister's new social life, shifted into high gear and roasted several chickens; my mother happily tended to various delicacies to round out the menu. Then at dawn of the appointed day I waddled out to Stelly's car, burdened with insulated bags made even heavier by dry ice. My mother followed, carrying hampers filled with bread and cake. Peals of laughter greeted us, and when Stelly opened the trunk we knew why. It was packed with food. Thus David and I shared our seat all the way to Cap Tree with the victuals that didn't fit in the trunk.

It was easier to find the dock than to get onto it, well below street level and next to the boat. Not only did the food need to be gingerly lowered onto it, but so did our mothers. Neither of them was wearing slacks, thereby challenging the chivalrous gentlemen reaching up to help them from the dock below. With the ladies finally in place after comical gymnastics, David and I hoisted down the food from the car to the dock. By the time we joined all the bags and hampers arranged before us, water had begun to seep between the slats and lap up the sides of the platform. We had to move swiftly to transfer the food and prevent its floating away.

Once on board, it became apparent that our mothers would be feeding lots of folks because many of the men had brought nothing for their own children to eat. It was a good fit because we had brought no fishing gear. But almost immediately after setting off David started to feel ill, began throwing up, and was taken below by his mother, who cradled his head for the rest of a very long day.

The men who ate well took me under their wing, teaching me how to bait a hook and play the line to attract fish. My mother remained aloof, though, unable to bustle about as a hostess or avail herself of the attention she could have enjoyed. Her blonde hair caught the breeze and her crooked smile drew men close, but she was socially shut down. When we arrived home well after dark that night, our mothers still had no partners. Stelly eventually remarried, and there were men in my mother's life, though nothing came of her dalliances.

A constant in my mother's life was depression. With frightening regularity—every five years—she would fall away and with equal regularity return, aglow with her knowing and frisky spirit. But I could never allow myself to enjoy her revival, regarding it as a mere prelude to the next, inevitable decline.

I REMEMBER

In the ninth grade, I would trudge every Saturday to see Mr. Glanternik on West End Avenue in preparation for my Algebra Regents Exam, the first and most terrifying of the series. I dreaded algebra all the more because my math teacher, Mrs. Newman, who lived in our apartment building and knew many of my relatives, had asked me to stand up on the first day of class, declaring that she knew me and it would make no difference when it came to my treatment as her student.

Her class was the last before lunch, when all the Jewish students cleared out of the school, leaving the Christians to the creamed corn and macaroni served up in the cafeteria by Irish dinner ladies. Since my mother worked, I would make my way to Aunt Marcy's for lunch, passing Izzy's Candy Store on the corner, where I sometimes had treats with friends, carefully avoiding the owner's creepy redheaded son when perusing the sweets or trying out a new "Spaldeen" for bounce. I would then stroll up the block, through the courtyard of 1181 Sheridan Avenue, into the hall and beyond the super's door, which was always ajar, assuring a brand of security far superior to today's high-tech variety. I took the elevator to the fifth floor, and just as I let myself into apartment 5L with my own key, Aunt Marcy would be placing my lunch on the table, as though she had radar.

The house always smelled good. I loved salami and eggs, potato pancakes, and salmon croquettes. Certain dishes, however, usually served with great fanfare at supper, disgusted me, like *schav,* a hazy liquid in which floated some sort of sour grass; *p'cha,* a rubbery jelly packed with mysterious bits of meat, garlic, and eggs; and lambs' tongues. Fortunately Aunt Marcy never tried to get me to eat the horrible stuff. All she dished out was mild amazement over the fact that someone could resist such delicacies.

Aunt Marcy also never gave me the feeling that she was squeezing me in, even though on Fridays her house was always on its ear with Millie, the cleaning lady, preparing the house for the Sabbath. A big woman always between diets, Aunt Marcy was inevitably swathed in housecoats and aprons when I would arrive for lunch. The chickens for supper were already out of the oven, and I was allowed to sneak crispy skin as well as any white meat I fancied.

On other days, if I ate quickly I would sit down at the piano and try out a new piece. She, too, would play on rare occasions, invariably choosing to sing "Kiss Me Again" by Victor Herbert. One day I heard honky-tonk music pouring from the apartment. Upon entering, I caught sight of Sadye Pear, a neighbor—barely visible through a cloud of cigarette smoke—pounding the piano, with Aunt Marcy gliding about her sunken living room. It turned out that Mrs. Pear, with piles of black hair and theatrical makeup, impeccably dressed but completely uncorsetted, had played the piano in silent movie theaters during her youth.

After taking my Algebra Regents Exam on a June morning, I finally emerged into the sunlight, already focusing on lunch up the hill. But awaiting me at the foot of the school steps was Aunt Marcy. She greeted me in silence, and I fell in behind her as she walked with great purpose. We crossed 167th Street, which took us out of our way from the regular route to her house, and entered a barbecue store. At the counter, Aunt Marcy ordered a substantial portion of spare ribs, which we then carried with us up the hill. The closer we got to home, the more confused I became about where we were going to eat because, although Uncle Dave was indeed fickle about his observance of Jewish customs, his home was kosher.

As we approached Aunt Marcy's building, I grew more self-conscious about our *traif* treasure. After leading the way into the apartment, she shed her coat, gathered some old newspapers, and completely covered the dining room table with them. Then, sitting in Uncle Dave's chair at the head of the table, she tore the bag open with abandon and let the wrapped ribs fall where they might. We ate them all, and when we were done, without being asked, I crumpled the newspapers tightly around the bones and immediately disposed of the evidence down the incinerator in the hall. Once back in the apartment, I noticed that Aunt Marcy had hung up her coat. With the table now free of newspapers, it was as if I were entering the apartment for the very first time that day. I then washed my hands and again made for the door.

As she kissed me good-bye, Aunt Marcy said, "Always remember."

And I still do. Her naughty demonstration of rebellion against her husband and affection for me was a good lesson in emotional multitasking.

THE FEUD

A feud in the family had resulted in the estrangement of my maternal grandmother from her two brothers. The loss of one, Allen, was particularly painful for her. She and Allen had sung and played in family musicales together, but Allen had resorted to forgery to steal a significant amount of money from my grandfather. She forbade her husband from prosecuting him and then suffered a heart attack. Harry, the other brother, caught up in the drama, had regrettably backed the thief. But his daughter, Hana, and my mother—first cousins—managed to resurrect their childhood friendship some years later. During the war, they met up at the USO, dancing to swing bands with soldiers on leave, but after my mother moved to Florida as a newlywed they lost contact again.

When my mother began working in New York after her divorce, Hana happened to call her office one day. Their rediscovered relationship, however, had to be gently presented to Aunt Marcy. Hana's mother, Ida, was still regarded as a surviving principal of the feud. But after Hana had visited our house many times my mother felt obliged to accept a Sunday invitation to Hana's home in Forest Hills, without telling Aunt Marcy.

Aunt Ida was charming as she spoke warmly of my

grandparents, remarking that she and her husband—my grandmother's brother—had actually been married in their brownstone on 6th Street, where my mother had been born. We shared photographs, stories, and songs around the piano. The lady hardly resembled the demon depicted by Aunt Marcy. Despite the good time, we did not stay late: I had school the next day, and my mother had a new job awaiting her. That night, though, my mother took violently ill with ptomaine poisoning.

When Aunt Marcy swept in after things had settled down the following morning, she became aware of our visit to Forest Hills. Like a crazed shaman, she lifted my mother by her limp shoulders, announcing that she was going to suck the poison out by kissing her eyes. She then flung her back down onto the pillow and left. My mother asked that I not tell Hana about what had happened.

With time, though, came détente between Aunts Marcy and Ida. As the family ranks thinned, they once again became acquaintances, enjoying chats on the phone and sharing memories. When Aunt Marcy's younger son Joel died, a reunion was contrived. During the *shiva,* Hana and her mother nervously arrived at an appointed time.

My mother's younger brother immediately presented himself to the nervous guests, prompting Ida to comment, "You've gotten so big!"

No surprise, since she had not seen him since his bar mitzvah four decades before.

TEACHERS

When I arrived at the Bronx High School of Science in 1962, the faculty was largely composed of Jewish women nearing retirement. In the classroom, they radiated rectitude and expertise, a combination that resonated with the largely Jewish student body. And, like many of the women already in my life, they had a kind of comportment that only enhanced their pedagogical skills. Many of us who had skipped grades were comfortable in this school, which was known for having no interest in athletics, no behavioral problems—unless being late for a piano lesson counted—and teachers with knowledge to impart. Such cultural homogeneity accelerated the learning process, and the lack of diversity was offset by a brand of cosmopolitanism ensured by a student population drawn from all of New York City's boroughs. That I became alienated from my own neighborhood mattered less than the adventures of visiting new friends in Manhattan and Queens. Even traveling to school on the subway was adventurous; within an utterly familiar educational environment, I was being transformed.

In Mrs. Epstein's tenth-grade English class, Sally sat in front of me. I used a fountain pen—an early affectation—and she wore billowing silk blouses, inevitably resulting in stained sleeves when she rested her arm on my desk, but she never got mad at me.

We were obligated to write one essay in class per week, which Mrs. Epstein would peruse as we worked. Mal, a fashion plate whose socks often matched his mohair sweater, had once made the mistake of presenting his essay to Mrs. Epstein early during one of these sessions, hoping for brownie points.

"A run-on sentence gets you an F, Mal," she pronounced. "Fuzzy sweaters and those socks just won't help you here," she added, having given him the once-over.

That she could be neither fooled nor distracted by the fawning fop delighted us, yet the prospect of such judgment being visited upon the rest of us was terrifying. Gradually, though, I started paying a different kind of attention to the way I wrote, even hatching a theory that by understanding a convention I could express myself subversively. Through comprehending the use of punctuation, for instance, I could manipulate ideas; thrown into the mix was a quote she once declaimed: "If you say something that has never been said before, it will never be said again." I got it in my head that it came from John Locke, but I've never been able to track it down. Courtesy of Mrs. Epstein, the words, not necessarily from John Locke, helped me stop trying so hard to be original.

We read lots, too. After studying *Silas Marner,* we moved on to *The Odyssey.* The established drill in Mrs. Epstein's class for the study of a book included a nightly assignment of particular passages to an individual student to be explicated the following day, but the level of personal classroom responsibility often depended on the liveliness of the discussion engendered by the passage under study. If the period whizzed by, one was off the hook.

The night I was pouring over my section I came upon the word *wimple* involving Ino and Odysseus in the sea. On a stand just beyond the foot of my bed was a copy of Webster's dictionary that I had been given for my bar mitzvah, yet simple sloth prevented me from consulting it. I even convinced myself that its context would reveal the meaning of the funny-sounding word. It gave me the giggles as well. At the time, there was a television commercial for toilet paper that featured a fey and bumbling supermarket manager named Mr. Whipple, whom I could not divorce from *The Odyssey*.

The class discussion the following morning turned out to be spirited, with Mrs. Epstein trying to get us over our irrational prejudices against a book simply because it was old and famous. In our minds, authors like Homer and George Eliot were interchangeable because both were dead and highly regarded by our parents. Then Mrs. Epstein called on me to read my passage from the book. She complimented the rhythm of my storytelling and then asked me to hold forth on that portion.

"And what does *wimple* mean, Peter?" she blandly inquired.

"Seaweed," I replied.

"It's good you looked it up," she commented benignly. "It's an odd word, and I cannot help but assume that the class would be interested in its derivation. Do find it in the dictionary for us."

On the short walk up to the bookstand in the front of the classroom, there was enough time to start feeling clammy. I read out the derivation of the word *wimple*—Old Saxon, Middle Dutch, Middle High German.

"Read on," Mrs. Epstein suggested.

After I had mumbled the definition to the class—the word *wimple* meant on old-fashioned headdress like a nun would wear—I glanced over to find Mrs. Epstein standing right next to me. She patted me on the back and thanked me for reading the definition to the class.

A year later, my usage of a reference book—rather than my avoidance of it—occasioned another lesson, one privately delivered by my new English teacher, Mrs. Berson, whose wet eyes and thick glasses were not enough to soften her withering stares. In preparation for an autobiographical essay to be used for our college applications, she asked us to write a topic sentence that would herald a personal statement. On the night before my lone sentence was due, I consulted my thesaurus because I wanted to get things right. I fancied myself lively and assumed I wasn't boring.

After combing through the book for synonyms and antonyms, I was able finally to write: "I am a dynamic person."

The sentence was soon returned, and scrawled across that largely empty sheet, in red, was Mrs. Berson's comment: "You? Oh, come on!"

MRS. ROOSEVELT
MAKES MY DAY

Our house always had three newspapers: the *New York
Times*, the *World Telegram and Sun*, and the *New York Post*, at
the time a paper of repute—the oldest in the nation, founded
by Alexander Hamilton. In the *Post* was a column called
"My Day," written by Eleanor Roosevelt, someone my mother
spoke of like a friend, in the context of the war, the United
Nations, and her courage in befriending a black opera singer
named Marian Anderson.

For me, "My Day" became a regular port of call. Although
I vividly remember Mrs. Roosevelt's photo at the top of the
column—a horse-faced and dowdy lady—there is only one
article I can actually recall: about why it was all right for
children to pick up fried chicken with their hands. It meant
so much to me that I fastened it to the bulletin board on the
back of my bedroom door.

On Wednesdays, Millie would come to clean house.
While Aunt Marcy saw Millie as a valued domestic, to my
mother she was more a knowing godmother, who, in turn,
regarded our apartment as something of a refuge from the
grind of being a black maid in the 1950s and 1960s.

Arriving home from school on Wednesday afternoons
was always startling, with the smell of ammonia immediately
bringing tears to my eyes. After a hard day's work, there Millie

would be, relaxing on the sofa and watching one of her "stories," shooing me out in the direction of the kitchen, where I would fix myself a snack. It wasn't easy, though, since the smell of the ammonia was most intense in the kitchen, where the clean floor was inevitably covered in newspapers. Millie believed that the stronger that smell, the better the job. I always marveled at the fact that the newspaper sheets never seemed to stick to the damp floor. Crossing them on tiptoe, I would make my way to the stove to see what Millie had prepared for supper. Nothing made me happier than a pile of her fried chicken.

On Wednesdays, with no cooking for my mother to do once she arrived home from work, there was an ease about her. She might pour herself a scotch and soda, hoping for a good chat with me. But having usually just played stickball, I would be hungry. And with Millie's fried chicken waiting in the kitchen I found it tough to buy into my mother's need for a gentle hiatus before the evening could unfold.

One such evening, after daring to eat our fried chicken with my hands and being reprimanded for doing so yet again, I bolted from the table and returned to place my favorite newspaper clipping next to my mother's plate. Upon catching sight of Eleanor Roosevelt's byline, she reached for her stylish glasses with faux bamboo frames and dutifully read the article as I sat there waiting for her to speak.

"If Mrs. Roosevelt has bothered to write a column on fried chicken and why it's all right for children to eat it with their hands, I dare not disagree with her," she gravely declared.

I was gracious in victory, letting a long moment pass before eschewing my fork and picking up a piece of white meat. Mrs. Roosevelt was now my friend, too.

Years later in London, I told my young daughters, Hattie and Tillie, that eating fried chicken with their fingers was not only all right but mandatory. That the English use a knife and fork for just about everything informed my instruction, to be sure. Of course, I cited Mrs. Roosevelt as the authority on the subject, although the girls did not know exactly who she was.

One subsequent summer at our home on Shelter Island a guest happened to mention President Roosevelt, and Tillie piped up: "Does he have anything to do with the lady who says it's OK to eat fried chicken with our hands?"

A NIGHT AT THE OPERA

One evening my friend Albert and I were dispatched under duress by our mothers to the newly opened Metropolitan Opera House to see a production of *Turandot*. Albert and I left 1235 Grand Concourse looking mighty sharp as we went off to Lincoln Center on the D train. We first stopped off at the Mayflower Hotel to call on Albert's Aunt Bea, a peppy spinster who had managed to live on Central Park West without burning faithful bridges to the Bronx. She took us to Stampler's and insisted that we have kiddy cocktails before our slabs of meat were served. By the time she saw us to the door, we were feeling awfully grown up.

Our entrance into the opera house both thrilled and intimidated us. We tried desperately to take the grand staircase literally in our stride, also pretending to regard the Chagall murals in the foyer as mere paintings hanging on someone's walls. Once seated in the orchestra, we were struck by the fact that we were surrounded by people speaking either with accents or in foreign languages. As if on cue, we began alternately reciting the lines of the fable *"Le Corbeau et le Renard"* by Jean de La Fontaine in the guise of conversation, having been forced to memorize it in our respective French classes. Feeling smug as we chatted in a European tongue, we noticed our neighbors chuckling. These polyglots, who actually knew what we were saying, had rumbled us—but the dimming of the ascending Sputnik-like chandeliers spared us further humiliation.

Soon after the opera began, I noticed the occasional echo of rogue hands clapping in the giant hall. Realizing that applause could be perilously misplaced during the performance, I took care to follow the crowd in showing my appreciation, determined to get it right. At one point, though, when the old emperor rose to speak—he wasn't even singing!—people jumped to their feet and cheered wildly; I joined them, though I couldn't figure out why.

Back home, I recounted the mysterious ovation to my mother while dunking chocolate chip cookies into a glass of milk. She looked over the program and discovered that the emperor had been played by the highly acclaimed tenor Giovanni Martinelli, thereby explaining the audience's outburst.

"Opera fans have long memories," she reflected, suggesting that they had been transported back to times before his voice had gone.

Now, a half century later, what I remember most vividly of that evening is the man who barely sang.

THE LILAC QUEST

*M*y plan to see the musical *The Sound of Music* along with my high school class had long been on the calendar; that it coincided with Aunt Marcy's surprise party was unfortunate, but there was nothing that could be done about it. My mother's apartment was alive with activity as I gleefully prepared to leave, armed with a legitimate excuse for escaping the day's chores.

Uncle Dave showed up to help my mother prepare for the party instead of going off to synagogue as he usually did. Aunt Marcy, his wife, visited us almost every Saturday morning, where she slyly managed to eat a plate of bacon and eggs despite her own kosher home. To keep her elder sister away that day, my mother had arranged for Aunt Marcy to take Lillie, a childhood friend, to a Broadway show.

On my way to the front door, I peeked into the kitchen and saw Uncle Dave arranging a mound of chopped liver in the shape of the letter *M* and my mother at his side, stifling an impulse to criticize so vulgar a display. Seeing me off, she quietly mentioned that Aunt Marcy loved lilacs and that it was my responsibility to bring a lot of them home in time for the party. "No sweat," I smugly quipped on my way out the door, a comment immediately matched by my mother's remark, "Don't come home empty-handed." She had this flat delivery that was simultaneously funny and disturbing. Then before she could saddle me with any further tasks I made a dash for the D train to join my classmates and the von Trapps.

I remember little about the show, its details obliterated by the personal drama that followed. Upon leaving the theater, I told my friends that I was off on an errand; I was not yet secure enough to confess my devotion to Aunt Marcy and the pursuit of lilacs in her honor. I assured them that I would catch up shortly at Jack Dempsey's—the nearby Midtown restaurant where the legendary boxer was usually ensconced at a window table. I'd figure out an explanation for the bouquets in my arms when I got there.

I spotted a florist quickly. In I walked, already imagining the enormous cheeseburger awaiting me a block away.

"Lilacs?" the man replied, his face registering disbelief. "You're about ten days early, kid."

Resisting his offers of other flowers, I haughtily departed, certain that he had simply run out of lilacs and wanted to sell me something else.

But the next florist delivered exactly the same message, taking the trouble to explain lilac season in great detail. Sensing my distress, he suggested that I go to the flower district, some twenty blocks south, in the event that a wholesaler had an early shipment. Thus began a tour of this unfamiliar part of town.

After I visited several florists there, the sun was already sinking in the sky and I still had no lilacs. But just as I was contemplating a confession to my mother from a pay phone, I located a wholesaler who sold me a trove of the precious blooms that I had come to hate over the course of the afternoon. Too late to join my friends at Jack Dempsey's, I was soon back on the D train, laden with those fragrant flowers. Feeling a need to ensure that fellow passengers did not know I had been to a musical, I hid the program within one of the bunches. That these were tamer times—subway cars with wicker seats, toilets that worked, and young children traveling on their own without parental concern—did not bolster my confidence when it came to matters of musicals. There was no way to conceal the lilacs, though.

At the entrance to our lobby stood Paul the Doorman, a towering black gentleman who knew my family well and was aware of the evening's celebration.

He confided, "Your mother's wondering about you."

Ever sensitive about her protectiveness, I processed the comment as pegging me as a mama's boy rather than simply expressing her—and his—concern for me.

Fumbling with the flowers and dropping my keys, I had to ring the bell. Before I could concoct some wise-guy joke about not finding any flowers, my mother opened the door and burst out laughing, delighted at my having accomplished a nearly impossible feat. Clearly, she had known all about lilac season.

Our big round dining table was brimming with fine fare—all catered food for which my mother mischievously claimed credit, even offering to share her culinary secrets. And there was Uncle Dave's chopped liver *M* in pride of place. The white and purple lilacs were swiftly arranged in many vases, their fragrance soon wafting throughout the apartment.

Aunt Marcy was indeed surprised when she arrived, wearing a bright red dress from Lane Bryant's. She made the rounds, delighted by the occasion and clearly touched by my mother's part in it. Though they were sisters, the two women could not have been more different, sharing little else than parents; however, so public a gesture was meaningful to them both.

Later Aunt Marcy sat girlishly on the floor, encouraged to do so by the guests' playful cheers that she open her gifts. That an old lady would do such an undignified thing startled me, yet here I am now, only a few years younger than she was then, very much at home on the floor myself.

And all it takes is the whiff of lilacs in spring to conjure up the warmth and hurly-burly that often awaited me on the Grand Concourse of my youth.

I'LL WAIT UNTIL IT COMES
TO THE KENT

*R*oy, my eldest first cousin, was elusive but always made people smile. Although he was my mother's nephew, they were close in age. As a little girl, when she was taken to the hospital to first see him she peered through the nursery window and saw him sucking another baby's finger. He grew into a notoriously naughty child, once leaping out a window, landing right in front of Aunt Marcy, and ending up in the hospital with a fractured skull. He also convinced his younger brother Jay that he was adopted.

Roy was drawn to show business like several of my other cousins, but he swiftly bowed out of performance and became a talent agent and manager. He and his wife Connie, whom he married and divorced three times, had three children, each of whom had exotic godparents, the most noteworthy being Jayne Mansfield, Sammy Davis Jr., and Helen Traubel. In one unforgettable photo, a beaming Jayne Mansfield is seen awkwardly holding a baby, her ample bosom preventing the infant from settling in her arms. Roy was even involved in hiding the Beatles on their first tour to the West Coast of America. There are photographs of him hamming it up with each of the Beatles during their seclusion in his house, where they were shielded from hyperactive fans.

During one of Roy's divorced periods, he shared a house

on Mulholland Drive with a childhood friend named Danny Simon, also recently divorced. Back in the Bronx, Roy and his brother Jay had been pals with Danny and his brother Neil, all four of whom had eventually found their way into show business—Roy as an agent; Jay an actor; Danny a comedy writer; and Neil a playwright. Neil's visit to the bachelors of Mulholland Drive inspired him to write the play titled *The Odd Couple*, with Danny informing the portrayal of the compulsive character and Roy that of the slob.

As I came of age, Roy was still working his quirky magic. I recall a trip to Los Angeles for a family get-together when I was teaching at Oberlin College. The prospect of escaping from a town that boasted only fine doughnuts and Buxtehude organ recitals was a delight. My joy was compounded upon arrival with news that Roy had managed to get us all tickets to a Bette Midler concert—no mean feat. She had only recently emerged from the Continental Baths (the cabaret and bathhouse in the basement of New York's Ansonia Hotel), taking the public by storm.

Prior to the concert, my mother, aunts, uncles, and cousins—Roy included—piled into a bistro for supper, our reserved table having more places than the guests in our party. Roy commented that we would shortly be joined by a new group he was handling. We had already begun to eat when some guys in leather, makeup, and feather boas suddenly appeared at our table, the shock of their arrival quickly replaced by the shock of their good manners. These bad boys should have been ours and not hijacked by our parents, who seemed to take no notice of their getups. There sat Roy, white wine in hand, presiding over mirth yet apart from it as well.

Not everyone was drawn to Roy's flighty routine and glamorous connections. At the height of the publicity frenzy attending the making of *Cleopatra,* when Elizabeth Taylor was being paid one million dollars and her extramarital high jinks on location dwarfed the pyramids, the phone rang one evening. It was Roy, who had great news.

"Tell your mother I've gotten you two tickets for the opening of *Cleopatra,*" he announced.

I dashed into the living room, where my mother was reading on the sofa, and delivered the news about the tickets, almost standing on my toes in excitement.

She slowly lowered *The New Yorker* and in a monotone declared, "I'll wait until it comes to the Kent"—our local movie theater, sandwiched between a Greek sweet shop and a mom-and-pop card store.

Before I could begin relaying an edited version of my mother's comment back to Roy, he chirped in my ear that he knew that she, more than just about anyone, would get a big kick out of such a special event.

But it would be a good long while before Cleopatra's barge found its way up the Grand Concourse, which suited my mother just fine.

THE BUTCHERS' DAUGHTERS

After nearly a lifetime in the Bronx, my Aunt Marcy and Uncle Dave finally moved to Forest Hills in Queens. They were late in leaving, long after their neighborhood had been emptied and refilled with strangers. The vacuum had been created by the flight of middle-class Jews who wanted to own their own apartments; what lured them away was a soul-destroying cooperative complex in a remote area of the Bronx, on the site of a failed amusement park. It was the closure of the kosher butcher shop, however, that finally drove out my aunt and uncle.

Right on the corner of Queens Boulevard near her new home, Aunt Marcy was able to catch an express bus into Manhattan. Although the subway was also readily available, something about that bus seemed to bring the city much closer.

Long after Uncle Dave had died, my mother, in poor health herself, often stayed with Aunt Marcy "in exile," as she used to refer to Forest Hills. These chalk-and-cheese sisters were suddenly visiting museums together, venues never before on Aunt Marcy's itinerary; even after my mother was too ill to venture forth on such excursions, she would encourage Aunt Marcy to by bringing exhibitions to her attention. Upon Aunt Marcy's return from an excursion, they would then pour over the catalog together and discuss the high points of her day.

Once, they noticed that Sir Jacob Epstein was soon to be featured at the Metropolitan Museum, an event for which Aunt Marcy needed no encouragement. Early on the day of the exhibition's opening, Aunt Marcy took a seat near the front of the bus next to a lady of similar age. A chat was inevitable.

"I'm going into the city to a sculpture show, the Sir Jacob Epstein Exhibition," said Aunt Marcy, casually responding to her fellow traveler's question about her destination.

The woman took more than a passing interest in my aunt's chitchat.

Rising to the occasion, Aunt Marcy began to embroider the import of her outing by placing it in a broader cultural context, saying, "I once sang in Town Hall, you know. Music events rather than museums attract me, though I'm not getting out so much lately. My sister is staying with me, and her health is poor. Did you ever hear Helen Traubel sing at the Met?"

As she continued to unfurl details having nothing to do with sculpture, she managed to sound rather grand, with a whiff of the martyr about her as well. Aunt Marcy then crafted a segue from Brünnhilde to her father, without lowering the tone. "My father was a kosher butcher in Harlem. In fact, my father and the sculptor's father, also a kosher butcher, were great friends. If I'm not mistaken, the Epstein family actually appears in the movies of my wedding in 1927."

"When did you see them last?" the other dowager queried.

Aunt Marcy paused and then proudly continued, "As a matter of fact, I was invited to the sculptor's sister's wedding, and that's the last time I recall seeing them."

The woman grasped Aunt Marcy's hand, her voice choking, and said excitedly, "Then you were at my wedding!"

The butchers' daughters spent the day together at the museum.

GRANDMA

*M*y grandparents took me to Radio City Music Hall the first Easter after we moved to New York. A mighty Wurlitzer came up right out of the floor; live lambs having something to do with Jesus walked around; and ladies tap-danced and kicked very high, bringing down the house. Then, just before the showing of *Boy on a Dolphin*, starring Sophia Loren—the memory of her wet shirt as she emerged from the sea is indelible—a Pathé newsreel featured footage of a regal couple, the exiled King Carol and Queen Marie of Rumania. Grandma grasped the arms of her seat, excitedly explaining that she had come from a place called Piatra Neamt in their country, though she had left it when she was only three. That is how I learned of her Rumanian heritage.

She must have been a very beautiful teenager when she married my grandfather and namesake. Charlotte and Peter—known as Pinky—had three sons: Fred, my father; Ruby, who was shot down off the coast of Italy during World War II; and Bernard, born with severe cerebral palsy. My grandmother was widowed in 1938 and married again in 1939; thus, the grandfather I knew—Abe, who was sitting on the other side of me at Radio City—was her second husband. The story goes that while she was still sitting *shiva* for Pinky, Abe—a suitor from the past who had lost out to Pinky the first time around—had appeared to pay his respects. Abe had read of his rival's death and decided to take a chance; just one year later, a span of time barely respectable in Jewish tradition, my grandmother married him. By then my father was himself married, and Ruby, who had disapproved of his mother's remarriage, went on to enlist in the army. After he died, the connection between his loss and my grandmother's second marriage lurked in many minds but was never discussed.

Abe was the sweetest of gents. Short, bald, and meticulous, he drove a black-and-white Plymouth, which was forever shuttling back and forth between Tremont Avenue in the Bronx and Welfare Island (now Roosevelt Island) in the East River, where Uncle Bernard was living in a hospital. He had become very much a father to Bernard, and as a grandfather to me he would sing, "I went to the animal fair, the birds and the beasts were there…," and teach me about wood carving and coin collecting. After my parents divorced, my grandfather and I spent even more time together, but in 1961 I lost him, too. One evening my grandparents returned home after visiting Uncle Bernard. As usual, my grandmother was frustrated by Grandpa's maddeningly cautious driving and puffed away on cigarettes. He finally dropped her off in front of their building, where she waited for him to park. Luckily, he found a spot right across the street. But as he made his way toward her he spotted a neighbor sitting in a parked car between my grandmother on the stoop and himself. Unable to resist a chin-wag with the gentleman, Grandpa leaned in for a chat on the driver's side; in an instant he was killed by a hit-and-run driver.

A widow again, my grandmother no longer had that loving cushion between herself and Bernard. His disability always seemed to come as a shock to her. Swiftly weakened by the solitary attention she thought she owed her vivacious son, she was obliged to spend much of her time on public transport dutifully visiting him. Her loss, compounded by Bernard's unbearable cerebral palsy and the exhaustion of commuting to Welfare Island, turned her inward. Our relationship changed, too. Convinced that my father could do no wrong, she became more his mother and less my grandmother.

When not on buses, Grandma played cards with friends. I remember standing beside her at a game in her house—beneath that chandelier whose crystals were individually removed and washed in ammonia and water—when she asked me to "wash the cards," meaning shuffle them. Not understanding her request, I was gone in a flash, deck in hand, and tossed it into the bathroom sink for a soak under the tap. The ladies laughed too hard for her to be cross.

Grandma also cooked pork, and I found out why. Although she had grown up in a traditional Jewish home, all religious customs had been summarily jettisoned by her grieving parents when her youngest sibling and only brother, Ruben—she had four sisters—died in the influenza epidemic of 1918. Years later, as an adult, I painted a whimsical floor plan of Grandma's apartment, featuring a formidable pig in the kitchen.

Over the years, Grandma learned, by necessity, to cope with her independence. My father was off in Florida, a shadowy figure in all our lives, and I was at Princeton. Bernard actually did the most for her emotionally, but even his ongoing support did not get the shopping done or assure her presence at card games and doctors' appointments. For that, she came to rely upon a car service and one driver in particular.

One day her doorbell rang as usual, but when she looked through the peephole she saw a new driver's face. She barked dismissively, demanding to know where her regular driver was. The man offered some explanation, which simply could not be heard through the heavy front door, further garbled by her own simultaneous commentary of disapproval. Finally, though, she was persuaded to open the door, safety chain firmly in place.

The driver, an old man, gasped upon catching sight of my grandmother through those few inches allowed by the chain. Alarmed, she immediately slammed the door shut, admonishing him to leave, but this time his words through the closed door were no longer those of a chauffeur.

"I knew a family of beautiful women…"

"Go away!" she insisted.

"In Rumania…," he said.

The door opened.

"And their name was Juster," he added.

There are photographs attesting to the beauty of the elder Juster sisters known to this gentleman long ago in the shadow of the Carpathians, and even as an old woman Grandma remained fine looking, and vain. From that day onward, Grandma drove only with her landsman.

On a whim, one day I drove into the city from Princeton, intent on calling on her before heading off to meet friends for supper. I rang the entry bell in the lobby several times and was finally buzzed in after being recognized by someone other than my grandmother.

Bessie, her childhood friend who was also her neighbor, opened the door, and I immediately knew that something was terribly wrong. Grandma seemed agitated and was breathing with difficulty. The doctor had already been called, and I was tasked with her immediate transport to a distant hospital. When I queried the choice of that hospital and the absence of an ambulance—What if I had not come?—Bessie summarily assured me that all had been arranged by her doctor. On our way out of the apartment, Grandma suddenly returned to her dressing table. She sat down, groomed herself, placed a scarf atop her head, and took a long look in the mirror.

I tried holding her hand in my VW, but had to keep disengaging our clasp in order to shift gears. I was also torn between focusing straight ahead on the busy roadway and stealing glances at her. Then, after crossing the Triborough Bridge, I caught sight of the faintest trickle of blood beginning to stream from the corner of her mouth.

That last journey was left to me rather than her Rumanian admirer. I had the privilege of carrying her into the hospital.

RED PLATES

*U*ncle Dave was a terrible tease who focused on children's weaknesses. Since he had married Aunt Marcy in the 1920s, when my mother and their younger brother, Jerry, were both under ten years old, they grew up being tortured by him.

In the 1950s, when my mother and I moved to New York and lived temporarily with Aunt Marcy and Uncle Dave on Sheridan Avenue, it never dawned on me that the arrangement might have intruded on their lives. All I knew was that Uncle Dave was irritable. Before long, his teasing found yet another victim.

After a particularly upsetting episode, I actually kicked him in the bum, shouting, "I can't wait until you're pushing up daisies!"

My mother sternly reprimanded me, but I sensed that her heart wasn't in it. The other adults present were more perplexed by my quaint expression about flowers than my bad manners.

Things did get better between us, which made sense given the absence of my father and Uncle Dave's sons' departure from home. Uncle Dave began helping me with school projects, his gruff exterior deeply at odds with the gentle encouragement he displayed at my side. Thanks to his influence, fur scraps often found their way artfully onto posters I was preparing for classes. Like his father and all his brothers, Uncle Dave was a furrier, though Aunt Marcy didn't own a mink coat until after his death.

In time, we became dear to each other. I came to accept Uncle Dave's religious idiosyncrasies: it was all right to eat Chinese food in a restaurant and watch television during the High Holy Days if the Yankees had made it to the World Series. I learned to live with his tantrums and illogic, genuinely appreciating his other qualities that made me more complete.

As he aged and developed heart problems, Uncle Dave reinvented himself as an "elderly gentleman." Once, while waiting for an elevator at his new apartment building in Forest Hills, I was approached by some neighbors who started clucking about a lovely old man. It took me some time to realize that their subject was Uncle Dave. There were still flash points, though. Aunt Marcy was vigilant about his diet, but for some reason his blood pressure could not be regulated. Finally, it dawned on her that the koshering of meat, which involved soaks in coarse salt, made nonsense of the low-sodium regimen that Uncle Dave had been prescribed. When she hinted that the routine of food preparation as dictated by *kashruth* might have to be modified to address health issues, his old temper flared, dashing his new persona. Consequently, Aunt Marcy assured him that she would not tamper with any ritual; though, from that moment, Uncle Dave never consumed another piece of truly kosher meat.

But neither a salt-free diet nor a religious fiction could prolong his life. One afternoon Uncle Dave set off for evening services at the local synagogue and died on the street, well short of his destination.

My mother phoned to gently inform me of Uncle Dave's death, mindful of my affection for him. It was only a few months since my grandmother had died. Now, in Princeton, I listened mutely, recalling that he had asked my grandmother's age when she had died.

"Such an old woman," he had mused. They were the same age.

In the morning, I drove to Manhattan to pick up my mother. We made our way to Aunt Marcy's house, where relatives had gathered. As though by secret ballot, they had chosen me, along with Aunt Marcy's daughter-in-law Myrna, to shop for the next day's buffet. We were soon on our way to Waldbaum's on Queens Boulevard because, according to Aunt Marcy, "their appetizing is the best."

At Waldbaum's we ordered enormous quantities of smoked salmon, sturgeon, white fish, and chopped herring, along with all the other fixings required for the occasion. Eggs and bagels were essential beyond their obvious appeal. It was customary to eat such food upon returning from the cemetery, their shape symbolic of life's circular renewal. Myrna and I then hit the paper goods aisle. Since we would likely be charged with washing the dishes at Aunt Marcy's house, we made a pragmatic decision to buy disposable plates. Discovering that only red ones were available, we lost our nerve for a moment; then, with jovial abandon, we started flinging packs of red plates into the shopping cart as though they were Frisbees, releasing ourselves from the gloom of our task.

At the register, as the cashier's fingers flew across the keys of her till, a woman standing behind us took notice of our large order of groceries. Arms stretched across her ample bosom, she nodded warmly as I piled up the plates on the conveyor belt.

"Having a *simcha* (celebration)?" she asked.

I answered, "Actually, we're preparing for a *shiva*," to which she censoriously replied, "Red plates?"

"They ran out of black ones," I explained in a grave tone, stifling laughter until we had pushed our shopping carts onto the street.

THE SECRET

As the only child of my father's marriage to my mother—his second wife—I had always longed for siblings. Eventually my father married a woman with children! Along with his fourth wife, Monna, came Jan and Jack.

My father and his new family lived far away from the apartment on the Grand Concourse that I shared with my working mother. Theirs was a splendid Spanish home built by Gabriel Heatter, a famous radio commentator, in the early part of the twentieth century, situated on an acre of land off Pine Tree Drive in Miami Beach. Along with Monna and her children came a wan chauffeur for an enormous Jaguar, a nanny named Rosie right out of *Gone with the Wind,* and various other servants to do Monna's bidding. I was thrilled to make cameo appearances in what seemed to me a television program about parents and kids living their lives with smiles on their faces, marred only by fights about bedtime and eating vegetables.

Jack was an adorable child who took his mother's breath away; maybe that is why I lost my heart to Jan, a little girl with crooked pink glasses and buckteeth who liked to drink pickle brine. We were both needy, I guess, and in the early days of my father's marriage to her mother a bond grew between us. We caught on pretty quickly, though, that we were not living in a TV sitcom, a shared reality that deepened our friendship over the years. I visited her at Georgetown, and she visited me at Princeton. She even got to know my mother, our relationship managing to trump parental acrimony. Once her funny glasses and protruding teeth were gone, she became a confident, intelligent, and svelte young woman who never lacked for gentlemen callers.

After settling at Vanderbilt to do graduate work, she became serious with a fellow named Jim, a divorcé eighteen years her senior. There was soon talk of engagement and marriage, to which our parents strenuously objected. The couple decided to throw a party for themselves in Nashville. When the event was demoted from an official engagement celebration by a parental boycott, Jan valued my presence there all the more. I was also keen to visit the home of the Grand Ole Opry despite my lingering prejudice against such down-market fare, secretly suspecting that there was more to life than musicals.

The couple met me at the airport, and I instantly became Jim's advocate, not seeing him as the "father time" figure conjured up by my father and Monna. We were soon at their apartment, which felt very grown-up, cluttered with fine ethnic art that Jim had gathered during a lengthy sojourn in India and on other extensive trips around the world. Jan seemed to be skipping a stage in life by becoming instantly established, but her happiness swept my insight aside.

When Jim politely excused himself for a moment, Jan

immediately swore me to secrecy and then confided, "Jim had a vasectomy eight years ago."

That one sentence transformed Jim from likable suitor to cradle-robber, and upon his return to the living room I marveled at how Jan was able to shift gears so easily from sisterly confidante back to engaged paramour. I was so distressed by the news that I was unsure how I was going to get through the weekend.

Jan's subsequent furtive comments about the situation reflected her conflicting thoughts. On the one hand, she had complete understanding of what his operation meant, yet alongside her scientific knowledge was blind faith that things would work out. In her own mind, there was nothing immiscible about wanting to be a mother while married to a man who could not be a father. I wondered if Jan had even told him of her maternal instincts. I suggested to her that Jim might explore a surgical reversal of the procedure, and that doing so prior to their wedding would demonstrate good faith in their future. She did finally agree that once back in New York I was free to help her identify a doctor she and Jim might consult.

Details of the celebratory brunch are a blur, but my memory of our journey that night to hear music in the boonies survives. It took a while to get to our destination, and when we finally arrived it was so dark that the outlines of the building were slow to emerge. Winding through haphazardly parked pickup trucks, we headed for a distant cinder-block bunker. As we moved haltingly forward, Jim offered assurances about the authenticity of the music. This was not some Nashville tourist trap with Minnie Pearls running around squealing, "Howdy," he boasted. We began hearing the music, and at least temporarily I was able to put medical matters aside, carried along by the spirit of the evening. The club was packed, with big-haired waitresses miraculously navigating the good-natured crowd, trays held high above their beehives. After sorting out beverages, we pushed further into the room, wanting to get close to the music, which turned out to be the work of a Japanese band!

Jim seemed unsure if he had lost face for having bragged that we were going to hear the real thing or scored brownie points for having dropped us into so absurd a scenario. Being comfortable with Japanese and therefore able to assist the performers, who did not know a word of English, and negotiate their way back to town just added to the folly of it all. If I had not known about that vasectomy, my sense of fun would have been unbridled. Still in this conflicted frame of mind the next morning, I left for New York, having sworn a pledge of silence to Jan.

I was now on a mission: to seek out a doctor who might be able to address her fiancé's chosen infertility. Despite my pledge of confidentiality, I turned to my mother to assist with the assignment. She was able to set aside judgment, kindly offering to look into the matter on Jan's behalf.

My mother promptly produced a doctor's name, and I

passed it on to Jan. When I suggested she insist that Jim visit him prior to their wedding, she would have none of it. The nuptials would be proceeding with no assurances about the prospect of children in her future.

The wedding was to be at my father and Monna's home on San Marco Island along the Venetian Causeway linking Miami to Miami Beach, with the garden on the bay transformed into a magical venue for the occasion. On the night before the ceremony, both families gathered at the house for an informal supper. Committed Quakers, Jim's mother and sisters were finely scrubbed and earnest people who tithed on a regular basis and did good works around the world. I recall one of them proudly telling me that they all slept on platform beds with thin mattresses, yet there they sat perched on overstuffed chairs in this opulent room, its walls groaning with magnificent art. But it was the wedding cake that became the centerpiece for the evening. Monna, determined to make it herself, had taken many posh pastry courses to aid her mission. She panicked late in the game, however, and ended up hiring a renowned French chef to produce the cake. The charade continued that night with her putting on a show of rolling out hard purple icing for a cake that would be festooned with confectionary grapes. To her dogs, roaming the stunning living room, she began tossing scraps of that icing, with the pooches going berserk as the sugar took hold.

The Quakers looked shell-shocked by this circus. Sensitive to his wife's hysteria, my father circulated amongst the guests, behaving more like an airline steward than the daunting figure he was. His temporary metamorphosis into an affable gent simply illustrated just how strange things were, with the bride and groom huddled together on a sofa praying to be beamed elsewhere.

Only one other person at the wedding knew about the secret: Jan's half sister, Margery. The next day she and I faced each other under the *chupah,* the traditional canopy, sharing knowing glances as we saw our sweet sister about to marry a man now cast as a wicked old coot. Not long after the nuptials, however, Jan told me that Jim had agreed to the surgery, and the couple went on to have two daughters. It looked as though my stepmother's audible prediction made at the wedding—"It will be a good first marriage"—would not come true.

In the ensuing years, family relations grew baffling. Although Jan had been outstandingly filial as my father endured undignified decline, she began to gradually withdraw from him. My own difficult relationship with him was not newsworthy, but Jan's fall from grace meaningfully recast family dynamics. Sadly, we became caught up in this seismic shift, leading to our own estrangement.

When our father finally died after a lengthy illness, Jan nervously arrived in Florida, shielded well by her husband and daughters. Monna asked if it would be all right for Jan to deliver the eulogy. Despite my tensions with Jan, I realized that my stepping aside might help her make peace with her loss. Nor did I mind being off the hook myself. The prospect of getting up in front of a crowd to talk about a man I could not fathom filled me with dread.

In the synagogue, Jan spoke her final eloquent words about him. She mentioned the marriage of *her* parents and *her* new father's entry into the lives of her own nuclear family, placing herself, Jack, and her mother back into a black-and-white sitcom. As for me, I was publicly airbrushed out of his life—like a purged Communist leader gone from an old photograph of the Politburo.

PROFESSOR FRANZ MICHAEL

Adrift in my studies, I was casting about for an elective that would fill a slot. I justified selection of a course on the Far East by my ignorance of the war in Vietnam, which was very much in the ether of 1967. Never a fine-print chap, I figured that such a class must include material on the war, even though Vietnam was not part of the Far East. On the first day of class, in strode the towering Professor Franz Michael, wearing a beret and carrying no books. With a lilting German accent, he began his lecture on loess, the porous silt that is blown by winds from the Gobi Desert and gives the Yellow River its color. Thus began his stewardship of my journey through Chinese history and the creation of a sinologist forever transformed by him.

As my commitment to Chinese studies deepened, I drew close to the Institute for Sino-Soviet Studies at George Washington University, of which Professor Michael was a prominent member. Like him, many of his colleagues were refugees from totalitarian regimes, having fled the Nazis and Communists and survived the terrors of Germany, Eastern Europe, Russia, and China. Their brand of politics seemed a natural testimony to past personal experience, bearing witness to current affairs.

In Professor Michael's class, the era of contending philosophical schools and subsequent dynastic dramas held my attention, but it was the Vietnam War that proved the foil for university life. Thus at the very time that I was grappling with the Confucian tradition, I also gravitated toward SDS—Students for a Democratic Society—and the growing campus radicalism that came with the educational territory in the late 1960s. It was not uncommon for me to go from Professor Michael's lecture on meritocracy in traditional Chinese society to an SDS meeting on the progress of the Viet Cong in their war of national liberation. The juggling of such disparate ideas, a rite of university passage, was given a sense of urgency by the ever-mounting body count chronicled on the nightly news.

Late one afternoon a friend suddenly rushed into my room to tell me that SDS had occupied the Sino-Soviet Institute's town house, chosen as a target for radical attention because of its alleged CIA connections. What I had come to regard as my academic home, with its books, scrolls, and porcelain, was now being portrayed as an arm of an unjust war machine. I then realized that care had been taken in concealing the plans from me, owing to my identification with the Institute. Song dynasty poetry had become the handmaiden of Lyndon Johnson's foreign policy.

I called Professor Michael at home in Arlington, where he lived in an apartment perched above the Iwo Jima Memorial.

"They've seized the Institute," I announced.

"Meet me there," he shot back and hung up.

His Thunderbird pulled up at the Institute, where curious students were gathering. Initially, there was little evidence of SDS occupation, but when we tried to open the front door we discovered that a massive upended desk was barricading the place. I could not help but feel betrayed by friends who had seized the Institute, yet kinship with the football players who wanted to rough up the hippies on the inside was inconceivable. Calling the police onto campus was out of the question—after all, this was the late 1960s, when town-gown relations were at their nadir. Professor Michael and I linked arms with my friend Ken, a member of ROTC, and a few others, in order to keep the sides apart throughout the night to prevent the jocks from invading and the invaders from destroying the books and artifacts within the building. If it had been up to the Institute librarian, Livia Jancso, no such restraint would have been shown. Her hair in curlers, she jumped from a taxi and was all for going in (Chairman Mao had been a librarian, too), but her anger soon gave way to sobs. She had seen books destroyed in Hungary and wondered how it could be happening in America.

With first light, district marshals arrived on the scene ready to serve writs to the errant students. At the same time, I noticed bodies wriggling down the fire escape and stealing into the dawn. The siege was over; there had been no violence.

As we finally walked in, a youthful faculty member strode out. He had refused to leave his office, guarding his papers through the night. Professor Michael had once quipped that this particular teacher saw Communists in his bed while he only saw them underneath. Recalling my entry into that building is still distressing. The library had been ransacked, the art vandalized, and the furniture smashed. For some reason, though, the cigarette butts that had been put out in the carpets offended me most deeply. As I crawled around on my knees picking them out of the rug, tears streamed down my cheeks. Professor Michael leaned down and helped me to my feet, insisting that I get some sleep.

Ken and I then left the building together, emerging into a very bright morning. There were people milling about in the sunshine, many of whom had occupied the Institute the night before.

Suddenly, one of them, a neighbor from Calhoun Hall, shouted, "Michael is a Nazi! He worked for Hitler!"

That Professor Michael had been a victim himself, forced from Germany's foreign service and his homeland because of his mixed Jewish background, mattered little to his accuser. It was at this moment that I lunged, only to be restrained by Ken. There we were, the New York do-gooder becalmed by a student committed to a career as a soldier.

From that spring of 1969, I sought the Way of a "true liberal," as Professor Michael described himself. I even bought a beret! Summoned to his office one day, I was told to take a seat.

"If you don't understand China's past, the present will

never make any sense. You go to Fritz at Princeton," he commanded.

In Professor Michael's view, F. W. Mote—known as
Fritz—had been the embodiment of the tradition I needed
to understand. Off to Princeton I went, happily taking up residence in the past.

When I spoke to Professor Michael on the phone and
told him breathlessly all about my new life, he could not resist
chuckling and saying, "At Princeton, everything after the
Ming is journalism."

Years later, in the early 1980s, when he was squiring a
group of Smithsonian dowagers about Beijing, I was living
there. We managed to go off by ourselves to wander in the
Forbidden City. Agitated by the pressures of living in China,
I was sure he would lap up my litany of complaints about the
police state of that time. Rather, much as he had done years
before when I was sadly picking up those cigarettes, he calmed
me and talked quietly of cultural differences that could over-
whelm the foreigner anywhere. It would pass, he assured me,
until it happened again.

We climbed up Coal Hill beyond the northern gate of
the Forbidden City to enjoy the spectacular view it afforded,
the very purpose for which it had been placed there. As he
bounded ahead of me, I noticed that he was taking some
medication, but rather than draw attention to his frailty I
complained of my own exhaustion, which gave him the rest
he needed but would never take.

We sat up there quietly, looking down at the palace through the loess-laden sunset of Northern China.

THE BUCKS

It was time to pick a topic for my senior thesis. By definition, I had to do primary research, but my Chinese was not up to the task. Professor Michael came up with a solution: to chronicle the 1927 Nanking Incident (not to be confused with the later massacre) from the missionaries' viewpoint. They had been caught up in conflicts amongst Chiang Kai-shek's Nationalist troops, Communist forces, and assorted warlords. Their records could be readily found at the Union Theological Seminary. He quickly had his assistant craft a letter of introduction to the librarian, requesting my access to the archives.

Immediately upon my arrival in New York for the summer, I presented myself at the Burke Library at the seminary in Morningside Heights. The accommodating librarian told me to pass on my good wishes to Professor Michael and asked for details about my project.

I obliged. Then overcoming natural reserve, he chimed in, "Might I suggest that you not merely consult the written word. Many of the educational missionaries who fled Nanking at that time are very much alive. Why not interview them?"

Delighted with this suggestion that might spring me from the confines of the library, I dutifully followed him into a cool, paneled room that he said contained all records relevant to my thesis. He then left me to it and said that by the time I was ready to leave he would have a list of missionaries prepared for me to pick up in his office.

After allowing myself to dip into several drawers of the card catalog, I strolled around the room looking at old black-and-white photos of Christian educators in Asia hanging on the walls. Some of the typed names in their captions actually turned up later on the list compiled by the librarian.

Over the course of the summer, the list steered me into the good company of significant gentlemen, amongst them, M. Gardner Tewksbury, author of an early Chinese primer of great repute; M. Searle Bates, a heroic protector of the Chinese during the Rape of Nanking; John Rawlinson, whose father had edited *The Chinese Recorder;* and J. Lossing Buck, a trail-blazing agricultural economist.

At home, there were books by Pearl Buck—although little else on China was in general circulation during these years of Sino-American antipathy—but they seemed fusty, belonging to my mother's generation. Early on in my research I wondered about Buck's relationship to the missionary sharing her surname. As it turned out, I learned that she had been married to him at the time of the Nanking Incident. I reckoned that being famous was no reason to exclude her from the interview list.

I started reading her books, beginning with biographies of her missionary parents. Inadvertently, their lives of faith, physical and cultural dislocation, and drama became a foil for the people I was interviewing and the letters I was perusing. Rather than dwell on the escape from Nanking necessitated by conflict between the Nationalists and the Communists in 1927, I began considering the China that drew them in, not the China that turned them away.

I wrote Pearl Buck a letter—she lived in Perkasie, Pennsylvania, a town in Bucks County—asking if I might call on her in connection with my senior thesis. In short order, an envelope arrived from a Mrs. Richard Walsh at Pearl Buck's address, which I assumed contained a secretary's brush-off. I was delighted to learn, however, that Mrs. Walsh and Pearl Buck were one and the same and that I had been invited for a visit.

I happily accepted and worked out a date for the journey, but getting to Perkasie was going to be a project in itself. Neither rail nor bus could get me close, and since I was a city boy, cars were rare amongst my set. But there was Lawrence, a jock from camp who nevertheless still liked me. Once, on impulse and much to his surprise, his father took him to a car showroom, gave him a budget, and said this was his one and only chance to buy some wheels. The only car that fit the bill was a pink Oldsmobile.

I called Lawrence and presented my request. Gradually peppering my spiel with tidbits about Pearl Buck, I got him on board even though he didn't recognize her name. Responding to his mother's annoying inquiry in the background about his conversation, he said something about Pearl Buck, and she was instantly beside herself with excitement.

When we got to Perkasie, it seemed like the whole town was an approach to Pearl Buck's farm. We finally pulled up to the house and were greeted by our hostess, a little old lady with eyes so blue that I could not help but stare. She warmly ushered us into a sunny room filled with flowers and summery furniture. I awkwardly fiddled with a tape recorder in preparation for the formal interview I was about to conduct. After cookies and lemonade had been set down by a retainer, our chat began. In the days well before President Nixon's diplomatic coup that opened China to America, being in the presence of anyone with real experience in China, let alone the winner of a Nobel Prize, was a rarity.

Pearl Buck's accounts of being trapped between contending warlords' crossfire and of enduring famine, as well as her puns in the Chinese language, happily derailed my determination to confine inquiry to the Nanking Incident. When we finally did focus on the subject, she presented her evacuation more as an inconvenient hiatus than a meaningful breach.

It was now her turn to interview me, asking about my family. I didn't get much beyond the fact that my parents were divorced. She sadly recounted that one of her sons was in the throes of a separation and that she herself had been divorced. She probed deeply about difficulties experienced while growing up under such circumstances, and I carefully parceled out information that addressed her interests. Her questions were many, but she herself gave away only one tidbit in a throwaway line: "I've never been married to a man who could support me."

Lawrence talked most of the way home, clearly in awe of a living legend unknown to him prior to our visit. He interpreted my own silence as canny insight into Pearl Buck, which could not have been wider of the mark. Rather, I was mulling over how Pearl Buck had managed to commandeer the interview.

Lawrence dropped me off at home, effusive in his gratitude for the opportunity to have made the trip with me. I could barely squeeze in my own heartfelt thank-you for his kindness. Back in the apartment, my mother wanted to hear all about the lady who had written the books on China. I beckoned her into my room and plugged in the tape recorder, but just as Pearl Buck glided from the topic of China to divorce, the interview suddenly halted—the batteries had given out.

Later that summer, on the day after Robert Kennedy's assassination, I took the train up to Poughkeepsie, where I spent the afternoon with J. Lossing Buck and his second wife, a Chinese woman, on their farm in Pleasant Valley. I had arranged to meet him at the local train station, and the only clue he had offered to his identity was "sunglasses." A sweltering morning, I was, nonetheless, dressed respectfully in my only suit and waited patiently until the crowd on the platform, all in shades, had left—save one. The towering and elderly Dr. Buck greeted me.

A courtly gentleman who seemed genuinely amazed that I was interested in his groundbreaking research on Chinese agriculture, he, unlike his first wife, did not wander far from matters Chinese. Yet the more he shared his insights into agricultural studies, sweeping aside the significance of his departure from China at the time of the Nanking Incident, the more I reflected on Pearl Buck's comment about no man ever being able to support her. In the comfort of his book-lined and shaded study, I tried to decide if the Nobel laureate and the scholar of agriculture had ever been compatible.

I went on to finish my thesis that summer, enjoying the seminary library more than I had expected, and the interviews with all the missionaries had been a privilege to conduct. I also got to play G-d by crafting Pearl and Lossing's reconciliation between the covers of my thesis, a happy ending known only to me.

FRAN AND JESSE

During World War II, a UPS man knocked on an apartment door; a young woman opened it and immediately fainted. Uneasy about picking up a stranger, he knocked randomly on another door, looking for help. My Uncle Jerry, then a young man still living with his parents, opened it and came to the rescue of Fran, a newcomer to 1027 Walton Avenue. She and her husband Jesse were newlyweds in the neighborhood. My mother, also living at home with her brother Jerry, became Fran's lifelong friend.

By the early 1950s, they had become my Aunt Fran and Uncle Jesse, long absorbed into the heart of my family. He was the gentlest of men, and she, raven-haired with green eyes, was a shapely and vivacious woman who babbled in an incomprehensible Boston accent. Prospering in the insurance business, they soon left the city, settling in the aptly named suburb of Lake Success on Long Island. I loved visiting them and their daughter, Louise, five years my senior and the nearest thing I had to a sister. Entering their home on Fieldstone Lane was like stepping into an idyllic TV program. It was a lively household, with Rina, their maid, working wonders in the kitchen, Aunt Fran bustling about with guests, and Uncle Jesse offering drinks. Before a garden room was added, the family would sit around an enormous table in the dining room, a Vlaminck hanging over the sideboard. Louise would immediately take me off to her room with friends, all the girls complaining about their mothers.

There was always tension between mother and daughter. Long phone conversations between my mother and Aunt Fran were ongoing, invariably centered on Louise and involving tears.

Mid-sobs, though, Aunt Fran would recover and go on and on about the perfection of her daughter, prompting me once to ask my mother why she didn't talk about me all the time—to which my mother coolly replied, "I prefer to have others tell me just how wonderful you are, Cookie."

Though I didn't understand the remark at the time, the simplicity of its delivery chimed within me. As the years wore on, endless dramas debunked my notion of perfect lives in Lake Success, but that didn't affect my closeness to Louise. We even had the same piano teacher, an eccentric Hungarian named Incy, who would eat green peppers and cheese beside me as I toiled at the keyboard.

Nurturing the enjoyment of music that Louise and I shared, my mother once took us to Lewisohn Stadium to see Ella Fitzgerald. A massive outdoor amphitheater on the grounds of City College on Convent Avenue, the venue hosted summer concerts of such renown that its organizer, the redoubtable Minnie Guggenheimer, managed to have flight patterns diverted away from the site during the season. The stadium featured seating on the surrounding steps and at tables on the field. We had a table, and just before the show began a waitress appeared, asking for our orders. I recall Louise ordering a beer. When it arrived, she pushed the glass aside and drank right from the can. That the image has endured alongside my memory of an enormous lady in pink radiantly singing "Mountain Greenery" is testimony to the impression it made. I guess it had to do with appearing grown up.

By the end of the summer between my junior and senior years at university, when my thesis was complete, I resented the need to type the tome, feeling that writing the thing had been quite enough. When I casually relayed my frustration in a chat with Aunt Fran, she offered to help out, informing me that she was a champion typist. I knew of her many talents: she had a gift for languages (she once began drilling me in French with her comical Bostonian accent), and she was a shrewd investor and fierce tennis player. But news of her typing expertise came as a surprise. Early the next morning I went off on the train, taking a change of clothes just in case.

She picked me up at the station, all business, demonstrating how seriously she was taking my project. After a quick lunch in the kitchen, we went out to the garden room, where the typewriter and stationery had been set out on the table. Impressed by her focus, I had the feeling the task would be done so quickly that I would soon be back on the train, but barely a key had been struck before Aunt Fran's pals started drifting in and the phone began ringing. Such distractions left me alone at the table, manuscript in hand, wondering when she was going to return. She didn't, but we had a jolly barbecue that evening. My distress at her lack of focus was quickly forgotten amidst all the attention I got.

Up bright and early and dressed in clean clothes the next morning, I made straight for the garden room, assuming that Aunt Fran would be eager to get started. There again I sat next to a typewriter and a nearly blank piece of paper in its roller. I was suddenly distracted by the garage door opening. In walked Aunt Fran and Rina, who had already gone marketing. Asked to help empty the car, I was admonished by Aunt Fran to stay away from the typewriter and reminded of her expertise and commitment to the task.

In the garage, I chuckled at seeing two tennis balls rigged up to guide parking in the narrow and cluttered space. Uncle Jesse had suspended the tennis balls the width of the car at the back wall of the structure so Aunt Fran could guide herself with certainty, the way pilots did at Hong Kong's old Kai Tak Airport by staring at a target on a mountain behind the runway. By the time I finished taking bags of groceries into the house, I noticed that Rina was preparing the kitchen for significant activity.

"We're having lots of Jesse's clients over tonight. They're all dying to hear about China," Aunt Fran drawled, on her way out of the house on yet another errand.

Back I went to the typewriter, poking away at the keys

and starting to wonder why I hadn't just stayed at home. Over the course of the day, I grew numb to Aunt Fran's comings and goings. A centerpiece arrived; deliveries came thick and fast; a glass of wine was shoved beneath my nose; and I was asked for my opinion on various dishes. I finally gave up and took a bike ride, deliberately finding reasons to pass Yankee pitcher Whitey Ford's house down the road, hoping for a glimpse of him.

I decided what mattered was that the thesis was written and not that it wasn't getting typed. I was thus able to be breezy about readying myself for the party, with Uncle Jesse lending me a shirt he had bought in Cuba years before. I happily chatted away that evening, casually quoting Pearl Buck as well as replaying Franz Michael's brilliant lectures on China. I did my hosts proud, and the guests stayed late.

During most of the next day no typing was done. Finally, by early evening Aunt Fran sat down at the typewriter, her fingers a blur as she pounded the keys. The comfort of that sound gave me confidence that my socks and underwear would not need to be washed tomorrow for yet another wasted day in Lake Success. I sat at her side, easing the process by sorting out my odd penmanship for her transcription. We were in full sail at last.

Then Cal walked in. A tiny man prone to circumlocution, he was a close friend as well as Jesse's client. Aunt Fran hardly looked up, appearing more a worker in a sweatshop than a gracious hostess. Her rude behavior left me to put Cal at ease, prompting a search for Uncle Jesse to offer appropriate hospitality.

The gentlemen immediately disappeared into the living room, with Cal gladly accepting a Pimms. For some time, I felt obliged to shuttle between the two rooms, blaming myself for an unfortunate situation caused by my interest in China. Once back at Aunt Fran's side, I remained tense, though also relieved to be at work. The pages were piling up; then Uncle Jesse suddenly appeared above us, his silence signaling his wife to leave the room with him immediately.

I watched as they moved together toward the front hall, where Cal was again standing alone. Once united, Aunt Fran appeared effusive in her attention to the little man, who was then sent on his way. The couple subsequently disappeared into their private suite, the house remaining silent. In the silence, Aunt Fran soon returned to the typewriter. She typed late into the night and was up early in the morning, completing the job by lunchtime, after which I was back on the train.

—

I went on to learn more about Uncle Jesse on yet another visit to Lake Success for a family barbecue. Summoned to the phone, he was predictably gracious, suggesting that the caller drive over and join the festivities. After hanging up, Uncle Jesse mentioned that a client was in the neighborhood. The gentleman would be stopping by, but Uncle Jesse confided that there was some sensitivity because his client's wife was nursing. Her concerns, though, had been addressed by assurances of privacy upon arrival.

Subsequently, the doorbell rang, and there stood a rumpled man with his ten-year-old daughter. When inquiry was made about his wife and the baby, he sheepishly confessed that they had stayed behind in the car, nursing in the garage. Aunt Fran and Uncle Jesse would hear nothing of it, insisting that the man bring them into the house, where a room would be placed at their disposal. Suddenly, we noticed a gaunt woman dressed completely in black standing in the doorway, not with a baby but with a five-year-old boy by her side, teeth glistening. They were immediately whisked off into a back bedroom.

The garden room table had been fully extended with many leaves, and all of us gathered round, with two seats left for mother and son. By the time they joined us, we were all enjoying a feast off the grill, with Uncle Jesse sitting at the head of the table benignly taking pleasure in the company of many loved ones. When the nursing mother, seated to his left, began speaking about breastfeeding, the table grew quiet in inverse proportion to the growing intensity of her rant about psychological bonding, natural immunity, and mucous, while her son chomped away on a lamb chop. She did not even notice that Uncle Jesse had slowly pushed away from the table, ready to take leave of the party. He never reappeared, preferring to remove himself from the situation rather than risk rudeness to a guest in his home.

Decades later, when Uncle Jesse was dying of cancer, I wrote him a long letter, recalling his handling of the indelicate nursing mother and empathizing with the indignity of his medical predicament. He responded approvingly, appreciating the link between that past event and the present, hinting, though, that he was now not able to escape from the situation.

In a postscript, he mischievously wrote, "By the way, that marriage came to an end. Even insensitive husbands have their limits."

Once widowed, Aunt Fran still powerfully returned tennis balls over the net to the wonderment of her young partners, became an even keener investor, and continued to cry about the sad state of her relationship with Louise. My own young daughters bragged to their friends about Aunt Fran's ability to play tennis at ninety-two.

Aunt Fran is now safe in sheltered housing out in Oyster Bay, where her breathless conversation and lively dancing amaze fellow residents.

THE DRAFT

By 1969, the war in Vietnam was drawing closer to me, with talk of academic deferments being discontinued. I now realized that graduate school at Princeton might not provide me with a safe haven.

As her only child, I was not going to be drafted, my mother declared. She had already prevailed upon our neighbor, a junior high school principal, to offer me a teaching job. That the only one available was in the math department mattered little. Despite having endured a lifetime of math tutors, I had to accept it, under the condition that I sign up for some education courses. I got on my soapbox about the sham of it all yet attended the sessions, believing that they just might save my life. But then teaching deferments began being called into question. With few options remaining, my mother consulted a lawyer who had allegedly secured a deferment for some famous orange-skinned actor. That his mother was an heiress had not prevented her son from being identified as her sole means of support.

We were soon sitting in the lawyer's office, my mother armed with a list of questions for him. They were dismissed. He flatly advised that I cut my hair and get rid of my mustache. Though I had gone to see *Hair*, and not dressed in a tie and jacket, had been at Woodstock and taken mescaline, urinated on the Pentagon during an anti-war demonstration, and listened to Dr. Martin Luther King, I followed the advice offered by the lawyer and soon looked like a Republican.

Weeks later it was graduation time. Miraculously setting aside their long estrangement, my parents gathered with my grandmother and Aunt Marcy for the occasion. I invited my pal Waldo, who had walked around with me all night in Washington, DC, the one time I had taken LSD, to join us at the Hay Adams Hotel for a celebratory luncheon. Recently, I had been introduced to vodka gimlets, and I was keen to demonstrate my sophistication by ordering one in the hotel's elegant dining room.

The waiter approached to take our orders, and my father courteously turned to my mother, asking, "Care for a drink, Harriet?"

"I'd love a vodka gimlet," she replied, inadvertently stealing my thunder.

After lunch, my father returned to Florida and the rest of us to New York. Then back in our own lobby I stopped at the mailbox before opening our front door, and there it was: a draft notice ordering me to report for a physical on Whitehall Street at the foot of Manhattan on July 21.

Numbed into silence by the shock, I followed my mother into our apartment. We went our separate ways, each of us disappearing into a bedroom. I took a good look around. I had just undergone a rite of passage in graduating from university and then received an order from the army, but I was now back in a child's room. It had changed little since my arrival in it years before, with its tweedy-looking decor of browns and whites, and café curtains matching the spreads on the twin beds.

After my mother and I had regrouped in the kitchen, before any mention could be made about the commencement itself, the charm of Professor Michael, who had shown up in his European gown trimmed in fur and wearing a jaunty hat, or the rare reunion with my father, I placed the draft notice down between us. In a moment, my mother, whose vulnerability could only be matched by her power, swept aside dreams of summer travel and autumn in Princeton. With casualty figures at new heights and the news from Vietnam darker by the day, in her view the sole task at hand was to keep me out of the army and alive.

My mother and I then spent the weeks leading up to the physical gathering all relevant documentation supporting deferment with military precision. We attacked from two angles: medical and vocational. Regarding medical problems, we recounted how when I was eight and playing with Sheldon Botashansky—the redheaded son of Temple Adath Israel's cantor—I fell off his bike and developed phlebitis. We focused also on the fact that I had had punctured eardrums, suffered a bout of pneumonia, and my tonsils had grown back, requiring removal a second time. Regarding my vocational skills, we prevailed on Franz Michael, a very public supporter of the war ("I can't recall refugees ever running north," he once commented) to write a letter to my draft board equating my study of Chinese with national security. His message was that during these days of no diplomatic relations with the People's Republic, when so few Americans knew anything about the place, my knowledge about China was all the more precious. We also assembled a portfolio including my teaching certificate, the job offer to teach mathematics at a junior high school, and the admissions letter to Princeton's East Asian studies department.

As the days passed, I felt that by the time of the physical all that could be done had been. Having made peace with July 21, I allowed myself to get caught up in the excitement of the Apollo mission to the moon over the weekend. On Sunday night, my mother and I went up to my cousin Jay's apartment on the other side of the building to watch Neil Armstrong emerge from the capsule and take those first steps on the moon; President Nixon declared Monday a national holiday. What should have been a treat, like school being closed because of a snowstorm, laid me low. Though never wanting the day of the physical to arrive, its postponement—a telegram came rescheduling the ordeal for the next Monday—derailed me, leaving me ill-equipped to cope with the resulting void.

When the second Monday finally arrived, I took the subway to Whitehall Street in lower Manhattan. I clutched the thick folder of documents attesting to my physical unfitness for the armed forces, along with those citing my importance to the future of Sino-American relations. But during the swift procedures of the morning there was hardly a moment to bring the file to anyone's attention. It was not until the last examination area that someone focused on me—and it wasn't because of a sheet of paper. Instead, it was discovered that my blood pressure was high. It was taken several times, with pauses between each calculation, always yielding the same result.

The fellow in uniform attending me said, "Please come with me. As you know, the army has the right to keep you for twenty-four hours. We need to determine if your elevated blood pressure is for real—if you know what I mean."

I was led to a darkened dormitory, where I saw rows of army cots. Filled with hirsute guys randomly stretched out, the place looked more like Woodstock than a recruiting facility. While being shown to a bed, I was told that someone would be by to check my blood pressure. I started remembering all the tricks I had heard about to feign illness, from the usual drug cocktails to eating raisins shortly before a chest X-ray to display symptoms of TB.

Gradually it dawned on me that with no mustache and no long hair, I hardly looked like the Janis Joplin groupie I was and so didn't fit in. I felt disloyal for having followed the lawyer's advice, unable to show solidarity with those around me.

A medic later emerged from the half-light, sphygmomanometer in hand, and took my blood pressure. It was still high, and, told to leave, I was up and out in a flash. The man at a desk outside told me that my blood pressure was at an unacceptable level for military service but that the army still wanted to treat me to a meal. I graciously declined the voucher for a neighborhood restaurant and got out of there fast, flying down the stairs in front of the building.

Then I looked for a telephone booth, fumbled for a dime, and called home. The line was busy, as was my father's. Next I tried my grandmother's number. She answered, and I breathlessly reported that I had failed my test.

Her expression of regret puzzled me until she said, "You've never failed a test in your life!"

When I reminded her it was my draft physical exam, she offered to call my parents and tell them the good news.

As my mother greeted me at the door, her relief was palpable, but, almost immediately, she expressed concern over my health. Clearly, I would have to see our doctor, but not that day, since we had to celebrate. Later in the afternoon, I answered the doorbell only to find Waldo and another friend, who had made a surprise trip up from DC to be part of the festivities. There they stood, one holding a bottle of vodka, the other Rose's Lime Juice. It was gimlet time.

RITES

The Chinese language was the bedrock of my education at Princeton's East Asian studies department. Thus, before getting serious about sinology, I had to reach a level of competence in Chinese that could be attained only through linguistic immersion. Courtesy of a Princeton-in-Asia fellowship, I went to Taiwan to study the language.

On my way to Tunghai University, I planned to spend some time in Tokyo, so Princeton arranged for me to teach enough English in Tokyo to keep me afloat. I was one of the "Princeton Princes," marketed that way by a Mr. Mario Sacraponti to snare grandees at the foreign ministry to study at his dicey language school. I remember little about him other than being creeped out when he showed me a photo of a stillborn child he carried in his wallet.

My friend Bennett and I had just enough money to stay in a proper hotel for a few nights. We dined out on *geoza*, the Japanese version of Chinese dumplings. It was possible to live even this well only because of the fixed exchange rate of the day— ¥360 to the dollar. After talking to other student travelers along the way, we found that all roads led to accommodations in Shinjuku, an area of run-down *ryokan* (inns). It was there that we eventually found a *tatami* room to share for ¥90 per night. That the place smelled of urine, was a hotbed of drug trafficking, and did not have a bath (we used the public *sento* down the lane) in no way diminished our satisfaction at having found it all by ourselves—without speaking a word of Japanese.

I could not wait for the arrival of my friend Jim, who had become a soul mate back at Princeton. Profoundly different from me, he drank quite a bit, smoked lots of cigarettes, had the kind of looks that I assumed entitled him to friendship with those far more sophisticated than my own awkward self, and then there was his fetching empathy. That he introduced me to Ken Russell's camp film about Tchaikovsky—*The Music Lovers*—and the books of Yukio Mishima, who was to die soon afterward in a ritual suicide, only burnished Jim's patina of exoticism.

He had visited my home in New York City and quickly endeared himself to my mother and all those who happily cluttered my life there. One evening, when the house was full of company, Anna Weiss, a mild-mannered neighbor and old family friend, let slip the word *wop* in Jim's presence. That Jim was only half-Italian and had been raised by his German mother did not soften the blow. My mother immediately asked Anna, well her senior, to apologize or she would have to leave. Anna apologized and stayed.

Just as Bennett eagerly went off to Taiwan, Jim arrived in Tokyo, and I assumed that one would take the place of the other at the *ryokan*. There I stood, proudly proffering a welcome in front of the inn I had found.

But all Jim said as he brushed by was, "We're out of here."

As a student, he had spent a year in Japan with a family, so it was to the apartment of one of its members, made available for his use, that we went. Upon our arrival in Yotsuya san-chome, Yoshiko, Jim's Japanese "sister," took us into her tiny home, giving us the *tatami* room and insisting on sleeping in the front room, which doubled as a kitchen. It was Versailles compared to the Shinjuku *ryokan*.

A rhythm quickly developed in this place. Each morning we would gather the futons off the floor to let them air on the sliver of a balcony. Then Jim and I would go to teaching assignments. I even managed to locate a Chinese course taught in Japanese. My fellow students, it turned out, were middle-aged Japanese ladies uprooted from Nanjing during World War II, who seemed to spend the sessions giggling behind their fans. That the class was in an old temple in Kanda, with its antiquarian bookstores, added great pleasure to my routine. Each evening I would return to Yotsuya, where we would decide what to do about supper, often meeting up with Richard and David, other pals from Princeton.

Bennett and I had not lived in Shinjuku long enough to explore the tenderloin; we were not terribly adventuresome. But Jim's familiarity with the place assured my introduction to its nightlife. We ended up becoming regulars at The Check, a basement disco with flashing lights that did not inform the darkness. There was lots of group dancing amongst friends as well as with strangers. Frankly, it was easier to cope with giggling Japanese girls on the dance floor than attempt to converse with them, but one of them stood apart.

Lala insinuated herself into our group, of course gravitating toward Jim, though she attempted to play fair by alternating between us as the music blared. Long after The Check had become our haunt, we were nursing beers there one evening when I noticed Lala's hands. Even after figuring out that Lala was a man, I simply did not understand how to process the information. In fact, it would take time for me to learn about the likes of Lala—and myself as well. Jim, I later discovered, knew all about such things.

He saw beauty in Japan and wanted me to see it, too. Taking me to the Fran-Nell Gallery in the basement of the Okura Hotel, he introduced me to the paintings of Shinoda Toko, and after many visits I happily bankrupted myself, spending seventy-five dollars on one of her prints. It has gone with me everywhere, a treasure whose presence in so many homes around the world has helped unify them all. Then there was our trip to Kyoto, where the beauty of Saiho-ji, known as the Moss Garden, lulled me into thinking I was in a magical velvet glade.

When it came to tea ceremony, though, I simply was not keen. Regardless, Jim insisted that there was much to be appreciated in a ritual that could not have been further from the rough-and-tumble of Chinese life to which I was attracted, and I agreed to participate in it.

We took a train to the home of a master known to Jim,

who had a detached structure on his property dedicated to the art of tea. By this time, I had grown accustomed to the Japanese environment, which made me feel like an outsized Alice in Wonderland forever bumping my head and getting wedged in toilets. Now I was about to enter a "Wendy House" that enshrined just about everything I regarded as fiddly. But I really wanted to impress Jim so fearful was I that his opinion of me would be lowered, and my prejudice against the rite was based on ignorance anyway.

We knelt as the master began wiping brown ceramic bowls with a little towel. He then poured powdery tea and water into each and set about beating the mixture with a wooden whisk. I struggled to engage myself, but the pins and needles progressively paralyzing my legs distracted me from the ceremony. Knowing there was no remedy for the situation, I consciously allowed myself to be taken over by the predicament, maybe the greatest testimony to the power of the event. The gentleman droned on earnestly, most likely about the magic of the tea ceremony. Finally, as though in a slow-motion film, I fell over, sending implements flying and transforming the master into a juggler as he sought to save the bits and pieces—and my face. But the worst was yet to come. I was unable to get up on my sleeping legs. Like a rag doll, I was righted by Jim, who gallantly hauled my flaccid frame out of the gazebo into the garden as I lamely waved good-bye to our impassive host. Off we went to Shinjuku for iced coffee, where Jim readily forgave my poor circulation.

The summer was soon over. Jim stayed on in Japan, and I went off to Taiwan. When we were both finally back at Princeton, we sorted out my sexuality in a room facing Dean West's statue in the courtyard. It could only have been with Jim. The resolution was transformational. But then, just as a pall lifted that I had only noticed after it was gone, he mysteriously fell away.

Vivid sensations of that time still occur, much like an amputee can swear that his limb is still there.

WALTER KAUFMANN

In 1970, I was a student in rural Taiwan; it was the closest I could get to China in the days before President Nixon's rapprochement with Mao Tse-tung. On the side of a mountain, amidst architecture influenced by Tang dynasty style and an early building designed by I. M. Pei—a handsomely severe chapel evoking the form of praying hands—I studied classical Chinese and taught English.

One day, I got a letter from my professor at Princeton, James T. C. Liu, a famed Song historian, saying that his friend and colleague, Professor Walter Kaufmann, would be visiting Taiwan and asking me to squire the renowned Nietzsche scholar and his wife about.

I met them at the train station. Barely beyond introductions, Professor Kaufmann announced his hunger. In shorts and sandals, the minute, spirited, and intense academic would hear nothing of staying in town for a meal. His preference was for local fare out near the university. All the while, his pre-Raphaelite wife Hazel, a painter, sought to curb his overbearing presence with a glance, light touch on the arm, or telepathy—leading him to simmer down, express gratitude, and still not give an inch.

Near the campus there was a hut with a few derelict benches and tables that served up a surprisingly long list of dishes, but where I only ate tomato and egg fried rice. I lived on the stuff, so delicious was it. I mentioned it in ecstatic terms to my guests, but the professor instead insisted that I get a menu. A torn and oil-stained sheet was presented after being slipped into an equally sad plastic sleeve. I took a deep breath and began a feeble attempt at translating the handwritten cursive script.

Mercifully, I was cut short. Professor Kaufmann would select his own dish, he informed me. He then flattened the menu on the table, closed his eyes, and circled his finger in the air before stabbing the menu with his digit. I leaned forward to see what he had selected. As though knowing I would have something to say about his choice, he held up his hand, putting a stop to any comment, assuring me of his fondness for all Chinese food. I desisted, shifting my attention to his wife, who sought my advice about special dishes. Of course, I recommended the tomato and egg fried rice, which we both proceeded to order.

The food came quickly, and before Professor Kaufmann was placed a platter of sea slugs. Without even trying to off-load some of those revolting creatures by offering to share, he ate the lot. Mrs. Kaufmann and I chirped on about how delicious our tomato and egg fried rice was and discussed the agenda for the afternoon. I still grow queasy as I recall Professor Kaufmann's telling performance.

By the end of our day together, Walter—as he insisted on being called—was convinced that he had gained a profound level of understanding from my irreverent and casual reportage as we visited old haunts. He assured me of a smooth landing when I returned to Princeton, where he and Hazel would be awaiting me. Such intensity, not uncommon amongst visitors who, knowing no Chinese, had placed themselves in my hands, usually evaporated as quickly as the train pulled out of the station. But not so with Walter.

Almost immediately a most gracious letter appeared from the Kaufmanns. In it, a chronicle of our time together was followed by expressions of warm gratitude. They went on to invite me for a Chinese supper as soon as my Taiwan sojourn was over. Not yet knowing Walter, I had hoped for a sea slug quip, but of course there was none to be found. Walter didn't make or get jokes, his enormous eyes wandering helplessly about when someone proved playful. I responded, letting them know my approximate date of arrival in Princeton.

Upon my return, a note from Walter awaited me at the Graduate College, saying that he and Hazel would be picking me up late Sunday afternoon for a visit to their home and then we would be going out for supper to the A-Kitchen, a local Chinese restaurant in an abandoned gas station along Route 1.

On the dot, he appeared in the shadow of Cleveland Tower and whisked me off to his home down Prospect—well beyond the eating clubs. The house was stunningly angular, swathed in glass, with images of antique Buddhas and leather-bound books beckoning from within. Hazel welcomed me with great affection, our brief but intense time in rural Taiwan leapfrogging the gradual establishment of a friendship. I had walked into a strange home that I was made to feel I knew well.

After I had settled in with some iced tea, a ravishing young woman entered the living room. I was introduced to Dinah, Hazel and Walter's daughter. With cascading copper ringlets bouncing about her head, she sat next to me, seeming to demonstrate common cause as her father then overwhelmed me with a commentary on manuscripts, books, photos, and picture postcards. She suddenly excused herself, only to return immediately with a black baby cradled in her arms. She would not be coming to supper with us, having to stay behind with Sophie, her daughter. Then, in an aside to me, she asked that I take her to supper the following evening and she would fill me in.

On that occasion, Dinah told me of her life in Cleveland as a single mother and hairdresser. It was no fun being on her own, she confided, but she knew that her baby's father was wrong for her. She was keen for a good relationship, though, and wanted more children. She also knew that distance from her father was imperative; she visited only once a year. She told me of her brother holed up in some ashram in New Mexico as far away from Princeton as he could get, and there was pride in a confession that she had not finished college.

Her frankness that evening and the few outings we had with Sophie before they left for Cleveland accelerated our friendship, creating a momentum that endured until the next summer, when she and Sophie reappeared. In the interim, I was becoming absorbed into Walter's life, starting to feel the ties that exist only amongst his family members. His intensity was demanding, but over the course of my graduate studies, as my confidence was gradually eroded by the rigors of academia, Walter's disarming attention was compensatory. This intellectual luminary always made time for me.

Every now and then, Walter would make wistful comments about Dinah's distant life alone. I had the feeling that even this daunting scholar had to make bargains with his daughter, choosing his battles carefully after big ones had already been lost. He also probed my regard for Dinah, and I spoke of her glowingly, but after such interest on his part became more focused I grew uneasy. Although the Kaufmanns were highly accepting of people, I never thought to tell them that I was gay. In the early 1970s, such matters were still not discussed. Rather, I learned to gingerly navigate Walter's inquiries while still maintaining a friendship with his daughter. Over time, our summers together became rhythmic rituals involving the whole family.

As I gradually drifted toward the job market, Walter generously wrote letters on my behalf to professional contacts at universities when rare positions in East Asian studies were posted. He was not my professor, nor was I in any way connected to the German philosophical scene, but he regarded me as a kindred humanist—and that was enough for him.

Nonetheless, academia was particularly brutal, and all I could manage were some one-year positions. After sadly leaving the second of my temporary postings at Middlebury College, I returned to Princeton to work on my dissertation, vowing tenure track or nothing. Despite my own sense of failure, confessed to the Kaufmanns by letter prior to my return, they could not have been more welcoming, buoying my spirits by telling me just how much my being back would mean to them. Of course, on my first night back I was expected. Dinah would be there, too.

I drove up and spotted Walter through the large windows, scurrying around the living room. Even from afar he was exhausting, the way only a relative could be; I needed to compose myself before the door opened. The constancy of his warmth, though, caused a pang of guilt, which quickly sublimed when it became obvious that he had an agenda for our time alone before being joined by Hazel, Dinah, and Sophie. Amongst the items on the list he shared with me was the preface to his new photography book about to be published. In it, he thanked me for thoughts on Daoism that I had shared with him. As I recalled, my insights had only been imparted casually, in the context of a delightful chat. Show-and-tell continued, long beyond the usual duration, causing me to wonder if everything was all right. Finally Walter seated himself, and in walked the Kaufmann womenfolk, the last in the queue being a pregnant Dinah.

Off we all went to the Chinese restaurant, with Sophie

now part of the crowd. It was an animated supper, as usual, and as we parted, Dinah predictably suggested that we get together the next evening. In The Annex, an Italian watering hole beneath a barber shop on Nassau Street, she flatly recounted how she had come to the conclusion that she would not be getting married but wanted a second child. In a practical spirit, she had then contacted Sophie's father—no strings attached—and become pregnant with her second child. She swiftly moved on in the conversation, wanting to catch up on my news.

Not long after that evening Walter summoned me to his office in 1879 Hall. Bright and spacious, it radiated a pride of place in the philosophy department. I came to understand, though, that its very luxury was a brand of academic purdah occasioned by Walter's aversion to analytic philosophy, which so absorbed and distinguished the department. It was easier for the best and the brightest to keep Walter in style than deal with him. As we sat in his sun-dappled alcove, he abruptly asked that I precept for him in the autumn. He dismissed my protestations of ignorance and fear and led me into an adjoining room, its racks piled with books. Walking down the aisles, he flung tomes in my direction, assuring me that I need only stay a week ahead of the students. Before I knew it, I was out the door and on my way with Hegel, amongst books by other alarming philosophers, in my arms—a relief, nonetheless, from Yunnan during the Mongol and Ming periods, the topic of my dissertation.

That summer was a time of variety in my friendship with the Kaufmanns, the ever intense Walter, keen to hear of China as I peppered him with sophomoric inquiries about German thinkers, and a very pregnant Dinah, Sophie, and I, appearing to be just another sweaty family ambling about Princeton. Then as usual, Dinah and Sophie departed in August.

As Walter's preceptor, I now saw him regularly on campus—when he lectured and for one-on-one discussions about students, papers, and grades. The gig added to my luster in the East Asian studies department. No one could figure it out, nor could I explain it. No matter. I was seen to be valued by Walter Kaufmann. Along the way, I also had the good fortune to learn a great deal from him.

We were now year-round friends, and I came to marvel at just how uncritical Walter could be of people he loved. His fierce intellect never obstructed affection if he got it in his head that someone was dear to him. While I remained daunted by his erudition, I stopped monitoring my own intellectual deficiencies in his presence. But with my growing inclusion in the Kaufmann family came recognition of Walter's cultural haughtiness. I wandered into the house one afternoon, coming upon Walter and Hazel in mid-discussion. She was animated in a way I had never seen before—her behavior wandering far afield from her usual application of brakes on Walter's hyperactivity. They had just learned that their son had become engaged. I immediately offered congratulations but swiftly realized that in Walter's view there was nothing to celebrate. He would not be going to the wedding somewhere in Brooklyn; the girl was from an Eastern European Jewish family. I quipped that I was just like her, but my words did not register. He announced that the date conflicted with a long-scheduled lecture anyway, making attendance impossible. That I did not let the matter drop, strenuously going to bat for his son and Ashkenazi fiancée, hardly seemed to affect my standing in Walter's eyes, yet his particular brand of arrogance did not sit well with me.

The year roared by, and soon I was again in the job market and Walter was still my greatest fan. I could not help but wonder what some evaluation committee in distant parts made of a dossier submitted on behalf of an East Asian studies job candidate whose most famous and ardent supporter had absolutely nothing to do with the Orient. I did get a job offer, and it was with the Kaufmanns that I celebrated the news—back at the A-Kitchen, of course.

Dinah returned that next summer with her new baby, and I went off to California, but ultimately the West Coast was not for me. On a whim, I then accepted a job at a bank in Manhattan. Even my defection from academia did not put Walter off. Rather, he expressed regret over my loss to the field.

Then, very early one morning, before coping with the rigors of my bank training program, I opened the newspaper and read of Walter's sudden death. The obituary recounted that he had forbade any funeral or memorial service, making his departure that much more frustrating by dismissing our need to say good-bye as we might have liked. I realized that by doing this he still thought he knew best. Those sea slugs darted across my mind, and I started to cry.

HUSSERL AND THE I CHING

These were the days at Princeton when black gowns were required at supper; students walked in a procession into Proctor Hall to organ music; grace was said in Latin by Professor Blum, the master of the college; and there was table service. Still wearing shorts or blue jeans underneath my gown, though, I felt freed up to soar with my pals, limits ignored. In fact, Proctor Hall was no mere ivory tower. There was plenty of romance, drama, and sex simmering just beneath those gowns; in the evening, the DeBasement Bar, a venue awash in beer, did its best to ape the New York scene of the 1970s.

Princeton's East Asian studies department was small. Thus, at the Graduate College its students were scattered amongst the more conventional disciplines. Fancied exotic by others, we were valued at the supper table as tangentially fetching rather than academically meaningful. While eating with the philosophers one evening, I gleaned from the conversation that the phenomenologist Edmund Husserl was flavor of the month.

The very next day, Franz Michael, my mentor, arrived from Washington to give a lecture. I met him at the university guest house, and we strolled to Jones Hall, where he would be holding forth. I tried to impress him as a renaissance man, dropping many names; Husserl's was the one that got his attention. He told me an anecdote about his father, a professor of English history at the University of Freiburg, who often went with him for walks in the Black Forest on Sundays. On one occasion, an enormous man emerged from behind a stand of trees and greeted the professor and his son warmly. Little Franz, then about five, ran toward the man and grabbed his watch chain, pulling at it playfully as he tickled the old man's belly. The old man was none other than Edmund Husserl.

Synchronicity was at work, to be sure. My lifelong obsession with Jung's notion of acausality had just taken hold after reading his foreword to Richard Wilhelm's translation of the I Ching. Hearing about Husserl in Proctor Hall and in the Black Forest propelled me to the bookstore to buy a copy of his *Phenomenology and the Crisis of Philosophy,* resolute that there was no such thing as chance.

At suppers I now moved toward the center of conversations with the philosophers, speaking about *Phenomenology and the Crisis of Philosophy* by Husserl and Wilhelm's translation of the I Ching, and feeling empowered by having the two books next to each other on my desk. Although the greatest of the Chinese classics can be notoriously perplexing, if regarded as a catalyst rather than scripture its imagery can be liberating. When it came to Husserl, however, I turned inward in ignorance. As time passed, my dinner partners came to discount my growing insights and excitement about the I Ching, far preferring to dissect my frustrations with Husserl. While feeling more and more marginalized by my mounting confusion, I became a spark for their own discussions, inadvertently taking on the role of agent provocateur.

It was at this time that I became close friends with Hugh, a Canadian mathematician. We would go for long walks after supper, chatting about everything except Husserl and the I Ching. Soon, though, we had focus: John Nash, a legendary mathematician often seen around campus in red sneakers and smoking an enormous cigar as he walked beside an old-fashioned Schwinn bike, and later the subject of the biography called *A Beautiful Mind.* He had taken ill as a young man, but he continued to enjoy unfettered grazing rights around the university. We would follow him, conjuring up scenarios about his wanderings and even copying down his massive equations and impenetrable prose from the blackboards in Fine Hall. At the outset of one of our excursions, we spotted Nash right outside the Porter's Lodge and followed him as he headed toward the grounds of the Institute for Advanced Study. Before our very eyes, he crossed paths with none other than Kurt Gödel, curiously dressed for winter on a balmy spring evening! Inadvertently, these strolls with Hugh replenished my energy, giving me the strength to be ignorant again with the philosophers at supper the next evening.

I felt as though I were growing antennae, newly aware of

things that were happening around me and perfectly willing to wait for them to make sense. On the one hand, the more I read Wilhelm's book the more its message chimed within me. On the other, Husserl's writings grew all the more remote with the turning of each page. One night alone in my room before my walk with Hugh, I could take it no longer. I threw Husserl's book against the wall so hard that its spine broke. Shocked by my outburst, I ran over to the two sections of the book, eager to repair it. Since the first page of the second half did not follow sequentially from the last page of the first, I assumed that some pages had fallen away as the book dropped to the floor, yet the pages were nowhere to be found. Then I noticed that the entire book had been assembled incorrectly!

With great ceremony and with Wilhelm's translation of the I Ching tucked under my arm, I dropped the two disjointed portions of *Phenomenology and the Crisis of Philosophy* into the bin. Right away Hugh knocked, and I babbled on about the meaning of what had just happened. He didn't get it, but the next evening, I held forth in Proctor Hall, much to the merriment of the cognoscenti.

THE PERIL OF NUTS

Anna Maria was a stunner from Chile. Too bad she was knock-kneed. Widely fancied by one and all at the Graduate College, she set her cap on Jim. Although he danced on the wrong side of the ballroom, she didn't get it, and he didn't mind. We were part of a pack that roamed the place, determined to appear erudite and blasé, although we never really succeeded.

One cold winter evening some of us stayed in the DeBasement Bar long after closing hour. Melissa, the bartender, looked the other way as the dancing continued and more beer found its way to her customers. When we finally crawled up into the quad from the underground pub, Anna Maria invited us to her suite for one last drink. Aside from Melissa and me, there was Maryk, a fey Polish pianist; Raffaello, a sinologist, clarinetist, and lifelong friend; and Bart, who had read classics at Harvard but morphed into a sinologist under the tutelage of Fritz Mote. As Bart had first arrived at Princeton knowing no Chinese, Professor Mote suggested that he go to Taiwan for a year of language study. His year abroad stretched to eight, and by the time he returned to New Jersey his expertise in Chinese was impressive. Bart chose to live in a local ashram, where he seemed to subsist on nuts, finding the environment congenial with his own Daoist beliefs. His patrician face grew gaunt, his eyes sunken, and his skin parchment-like, undoubtedly due to the diet.

Anna Maria's suite was off the back courtyard of the Graduate College, a good distance from the bar. Because her roommate was asleep in the adjoining room, the music she played on her Victrola was barely audible. In such quiet surroundings, the clinking ice cubes seemed deafening as we made small talk. Meanwhile, the nuts from Bart's diet must have been at work; with a Daoist sense of abandon, he suddenly unleashed a thunderous fart, its noise blowing all decorum to smithereens. Not surprisingly, the party soon broke up. On our way out, I was still in stitches.

He sidled up to me and asked, "Do you think I've ruined my chances with Anna Maria?"

A BIRD IN THE FACE

I wanted out of the dorm, and Professor James Liu happened to mention that his colleague, Kenneth Ch'en, Princeton's renowned scholar of Chinese Buddhism, needed a house sitter. Professor Ch'en, a recent widower, was shortly bound for California to look into a visiting professorship. I could live in his house as a caretaker while he traveled, and I was obliged only to pick him up at the airport when he occasionally visited and lay low when he was in residence.

Professor Ch'en's nondescript home was noteworthy in a neighborhood of architecturally bold faculty housing alongside Butler, a compound of old bungalows used mostly by married students. On my way there to meet him, I passed the elegant home of the Motes, which had been fashioned after a traditional Japanese farmhouse and surrounded by rogue bamboo. I had once pulled up to the periphery of the property armed with a shovel, to dig up bamboo roots so I could grow the plants in my dorm room. At the time of my adventure, the Motes were on sabbatical in Colorado and the house was empty. There I was, stamping on the top of the shovel, totally focused on cutting through a section of the notoriously tenacious roots, when a car halted at the curb, its laughing occupants sending wolf whistles in my direction. Then I noticed that my jeans had slipped down, providing an ample view of my briefs.

As I approached the front door of the Ch'en house, I heard a TV blaring. I rang the bell, but no one answered. I pounded but still got no answer. Finally, a tiny, older man appeared before me, startled. It was Professor Ch'en. Shouting some sort of greeting above the television, he waved me into the house.

As I scanned the interior, I noticed the *Britannica* on book shelves otherwise empty. Perched on a stand in the entry hall was a stuffed animal—not the children's variety but some sort of rodent mounted by a taxidermist. The living room had little furniture, save an enormous reclining chair set squarely in front of the TV. He returned to his basketball game, barely paying me any mind. He barked that he didn't need transport to Newark Airport when he would be leaving in a few days on a quick trip, and I could move in right after he left. He then handed me the house keys and said he'd be in touch about the details of his return. On my way out, I noticed several envelopes from the Republican Party on a table along-side the rodent. Driving off, I felt dismayed by the evidence that this esteemed scholar was a Republican basketball fan who lived with no books and a stuffed rat.

Soon after, I moved in, and having been a lifelong apartment-dweller I enjoyed the novelty of living in a house. Liberated from the dorm, I could actually cook meals for friends. My first guest would be Jim.

"Can I bring Rob along?" he asked on the day of our supper.

Though I did not know Rob, I extended the invitation to include him.

Rather proud of my new digs, I prepared a special meal. a hollowed-out round rye bread filled with Swedish meatballs, a recipe that included grape jelly, which was critical to its success. Fresh vegetables were on offer as well. At supper, Rob made a rude comment about the succotash, which wounded me. I could only imagine what he would have said if he had known about the grape jelly. Mysteriously overreacting, I casually excused myself, made for the top drawer in my bedroom bureau, took out a small wooden box carved by my grandfather, located a dog-eared envelope with the last of my Woodstock stash of mescaline, popped the pill in my mouth, and rejoined my guests. The secret pleasure of having ingested that pill, even before it started working, got me through the rest of the evening.

But the effects of the mescaline weren't as I had remembered them at Woodstock. As the night wore on, I became obsessed with trying to open the window above my bed, unable to understand why it could not be done. In the morning I realized that what I had taken for a window was actually a reflection generated by a streetlight outside the real window, which was next to my bed. It struck me that there must have been few mushrooms and lots of speed in the pill I had taken. I had to function, however, as I was due at Newark Airport to pick up Professor Ch'en. Off I sped in my Beetle, singing loudly along with the blaring radio, up the New Jersey Turnpike. The music and wide-open windows restored my sense of well-being.

Professor Ch'en hardly seemed the man I had recently met. He returned as a smitten teenager, accompanied by Mrs. Mok, a wizened Chinese librarian, on his arm. On the drive home, I refrained from playing the radio, but the floor show in the rearview mirror made up for it. I watched the librarian's fingers fiddling with the nape of his neck. He admonished me to drive slowly, the speed of the car prolonging the massage, perhaps. Then passing drivers began blowing their horns and making hostile gestures in our direction. Professor Ch'en and Mrs. Mok did not take any notice at first, until a car pulled up on the passenger side. The driver rolled down his window and flipped him the bird. Startled, Professor Ch'en barked something in Chinese; then, looking around, he sought some sort of explanation. I shrugged, baffled by the episode. After several more miles on the turnpike, the penny dropped. The bombing of Cambodia during President Nixon's expansion of the war in Vietnam had set off demonstrations on campus. In the heat of such political indignation, I had drawn a sign reading, "Strike," with pretentious Chinese characters for it—*ba-ke*—atop the English, and fastened it to the back of the car to express solidarity with the anti-war movement. Even though I now knew the reason for the road rage aimed at us, I was obliged to appear ignorant. Panic set in when I began thinking of the driveway leading up to Professor Ch'en's front door. If I were to approach the house as usual, which would place the rear of the car facing the front door, he could not miss the inflammatory placard on the back of the car. I saw myself being summarily evicted and banished to a dormitory if I didn't figure out a way to get up the driveway without the sign being seen.

Abuse continued until we left the turnpike. Once back in Princeton, hostility turned to warmth, with people waving at us as we progressed along Nassau Street and down Washington Road. Professor Ch'en chose to cite to his companion such public displays of hospitality as a reason for her to spend lots of time with him in Princeton.

To distract him in advance of my parking maneuver, I started chattering about my admiration for his ability to whiz through documents written in Pali, the language of Buddhist scriptures.

"Not a problem," he modestly commented.

Evidently, my mention of texts and Mrs. Mok's resumed attention to his nape prompted him to offer a lively account of his recent research in California.

As we came to the driveway, I mentioned a problem with the windshield wipers, requiring strong light to investigate— the light at the front door would be just perfect. Thus, I justified a ridiculous maneuver that placed the front of the car right under the beam. Professor Ch'en hopped out, never seeing the sign. He then entered the house, leaving Mrs. Mok and me on the doorstep. I saw her in, with relief over my deception immediately giving way to a crisis of conscience about whether I should have owned up to the sign. But I took comfort in the fact that his neighbors might catch sight of the placard as I went about my business, thinking that the great Kenneth Ch'en had finally seen the light.

TAMINO'S GIFTS

There was no way I was going back to the dorm after my time was up at Professor Chen's house. I put out the word amongst my friends with inroads into the "grande dame circuit" to find me a house-sitting sinecure in Princeton. In my mind, I had contrived a link between my environment and the ability to work seriously on my dissertation.

Bobbie, a horse-mad graduate student, alerted me to an opportunity. Alison Frantz, an eminent archaeologist, had to make a sudden trip to Greece, and her house and cat needed looking after. I was to show up at 3:00 the next afternoon at a house on Haslet Avenue, nestled between the Graduate College and the Institute for Advanced Study.

At the appointed time, I cycled up to a low-slung home made of cinder block, musing that I had never noticed it in all the years I had been riding my bike in this neighborhood. A car and driver were in front of the house, and an elderly lady, with a wig not quite straight on her head, stood near the footpath. Before I could even inquire if she was Miss Alison Frantz, the front door opened and out came another old lady, bearing a suitcase and a chiseled scowl. Though feeling discourteous not to run toward her and offer to take her bag, I was fixed to my spot by the sense of command and capability she exuded.

When she approached me, she put down her bag and reached into her no-nonsense pocketbook, dropped her keys into my hand, and said, "If there's a fire, save the cat." Then she was gone.

The first lady introduced herself as Janet Cottier, Miss Frantz's sister. She pounded me on my chest and barked, "Come along, Dearie."

Up the path we walked on pebbled concrete, which continued through the house. The interior could not have been in greater contrast to the cinder-block exterior. Angular and dramatic, the great room was lined in wood and brick, the floors covered in cork, with the bumpy path leading outside to a garden room and then to a guest house. As she strode through, Mrs. Cottier dismissed the room as too dark, a place where her flowers would simply not last.

"It's the cat that requires your attention," she stated, brusquely diverting my wandering eyes with a gnarled finger toward another room where the animal I was to save could be found if the place went up in flames.

I followed in the wake of her long, heavy strides to find Tamino, a Manx, curled up at the foot of Miss Frantz's bed.

"Each morning, when Tamino awakens you, you must prepare either fresh prawns or kidneys for his breakfast," she commanded. "No need to worry about shopping. Provisions will be delivered regularly by the butcher. You mustn't freeze them."

Turning on her heels, she exited the room. While she

took her sisterly obligations seriously, she seemed to have little time for a cat that warranted such treatment. For my part, I felt queasy about handling seafood and offal at dawn.

She then led me to the front hall to show me how to disable the burglar alarm.

"You'd best pay attention because the chaps will come with guns drawn if you get it wrong. It's a silent alarm right to the police station," she admonished.

Next she took me to the screened-in garden room opposite the guest house and suggested that we sit down for a chat. She had done some homework, showing informed interest in my studies, family, and travels. Then I asked a bit about her. She first spoke warmly of her garden and needlepoint and then abruptly shifted gears to Ham, her husband, describing him as someone who annotated books in his library all day. What really enlivened her were her own Cavalier King Charles Spaniels, Robbie and Goblin. I wondered what she fed her pooches at dawn.

Pointing to a big house at the top of the garden behind a wall, she told me that she and her siblings had grown up there. That property fronted onto Battle Road, which her mother had gotten renamed as the site of military action in the American Revolution. In her will she had left the back lot— then an apple orchard—to Alison, on which to build this house.

Their mother, an émigré to America from the Outer Hebrides, had moved to Duluth and married a wealthy newspaper publisher. Widowed at a very young age with five children and determined to plant herself near a fine university, she toured college towns along the East Coast, finally coming to rest in Princeton. The family temporarily lived in Bainbridge House, between PJ's Pancake House and the Garden Theater on Nassau Street. The house later became the town library and finally the historical society.

After Mrs. Cottier left, I discovered a maid's room atop the kitchen and a passageway running parallel to the front of the house. Miss Frantz's darkroom—she was not only an archaeologist but a photographer of antiquities—occupied the entire upper level over the two ground-floor bedrooms, which were joined by two bathrooms. On many of the walls were austere and artful black-and-white photographs, not of Grecian urns but rather of quirky scenes, including one of a cat in a fig tree.

Eventually I focused on Tamino, who infuriated me by being elusive. I lay on Miss Frantz's bed for a while before he appeared and briefly looked me over. He then made his way out to a basket on the porch, and I dutifully followed. My training had begun.

On the first night of my occupancy, I had planned to meet friends, including Bobbie, who had made all this happen. But before I could leave for The Annex, I had to look after Tamino. Despite my antipathy toward the animal, I felt responsible for his safety. After all, Miss Frantz had entrusted her feline-centric establishment to me—rent free. I dutifully awaited the cat's return from dusk maneuvers before setting off.

After getting grilled about the house by the folks around the table, I also learned a great deal about Miss Frantz. Evidently, she had been a spy in Greece during World War II, as well as the partner of the late Lucy Talcott, with whom she had collaborated on the excavation of the Agora. I suddenly understood the layout of the house. Their living quarters were secreted beyond a massive wooden pocket door, just the thing for the privacy warranted by a Boston marriage. It was said that Miss Talcott could date shards by tasting them.

A rhythm quickly governed my life, largely imposed by Tamino. I soon gave up grumbling about his slimy dawn fare and got an early start pedaling off in the still-cool mornings to Firestone and Gest libraries, where I grappled with texts on Yunnan. But there was more to life than primary sources and a cat that summer.

There was Ricky, the younger brother of a student at Middlebury, where I had been teaching. He was the runt of four brothers, and his family, much to my surprise, had been close to my Uncle Bernard via a camp for the handicapped where he had often spent his summers. I met Ricky after my tap-dancing solo in top hat and tights at the Middlebury commencement recital. Some weeks after that flimsy introduction, he presented himself at Miss Frantz's house. During his unexpectedly lengthy stay, there was lots of swimming and many walks through the Institute woods. While memories of water and strolls still glisten through the years, it was Mrs. Cottier who stole the show.

At the outset of my sojourn in Miss Frantz's house, Mrs. Cottier was both laissez-faire and meddling. She seemed to know just when the cat had been fed, ringing me for a supposedly casual chat. During its course, she was able to not only confirm the cat's well-being but also check up on the butcher's deliveries, appropriate use of the food, and anything else she chose to discuss. At first, I resented her intrusions, but as those early days drifted by, her calls became less predictable. Their content shifted from the cat, revealing her Democratic politics (she grudgingly mentioned her sister, Barbara, the Republican, who was visiting from Philadelphia), and her sense of mirth (she recounted how her next door neighbor, Pepper Constable, always rode his lawnmower in a jacket and tie) to righteous indignation (she asked, "Whoever heard of guitar-playing in a chapel?").

One steamy afternoon I impulsively bought some ice cream and cycled over to her home at 4 Orchard Circle, right behind Lowrie House, the president's residence. It took a long time for someone to come to the front door. When it finally opened, I could hear Mrs. Cottier's voice, none too pleased by the disturbance. Meekly offering up my ice cream, I barely caught sight of her as she reached out to accept the package. Some polite noises were made, and then the door was shut. I returned home crestfallen at my chilly reception, but just as I entered the house the phone rang. It was Mrs. Cottier insisting that I call her Janet and come for supper that evening.

During this meal, I learned that in Janet's home afternoon naps were sacred, coffee was never served, and evenings ended at 9:15 pm. I also met Ham, who could, indeed, usually be found in his library, a bridge between the main house and "the wing"—a granny flat atop the garage. The son of Baltimore socialites, he had grown up in the Plaza Hotel, "read English" at Princeton and Oxford, and never completed his PhD on Walter Scott, which must have accounted for his compulsive writing of marginalia in the rare books to be found in his library. In fact, years later, when wavering about the completion of my own doctorate, I thought of Ham and determined that no version of his fate would be mine.

Now that Ham was in his dotage, it was hard to get a sense of his relationship with Janet. He could not now be the man she married. I later discovered that he was not even the man she had *wanted* to marry. Evidently, she had fallen in love with a Princeton undergraduate and Scottish peer named Peter. Although Janet's mother was a well-heeled and upright Scot herself, Peter's mother disapproved and summoned him home to Scotland. On the rebound, Janet took up with Ham, and they soon became engaged. Subsequently, Peter returned to Princeton, defying his family and fully expecting to begin a life with Janet, only to find her spoken for. It was the road not taken which, I suspect, informed the rest of her life with Ham.

Though both Janet and Peter married others, they quietly met regularly in London over the years, with one of Janet's nieces acting as her beard on these trips. The romance ended suddenly when Peter died sculling on the Thames in the 1950s, and as Janet told me years later while we sipped gin and tonics on her patio, she felt she, too, had died on that day so long ago. She also confessed that she always had a soft spot for me because my name was Peter.

There were other suppers at Janet's that summer, as well as early morning visits from her, giving me a chance to get to know her well. I had by now willingly accommodated myself to Tamino's routine, grateful for the chance to live in a magical house. One evening I had hoped that Tamino would return a bit earlier from his late afternoon adventures so I could leave for supper at a friend's house. But he did not, so I called Janet, asking her advice.

"Go off to your friend's house," she commanded.

Had one of her own animals gone AWOL, I could not help but wonder if she would have been so cavalier, but off I went, backing out of the driveway onto Haslet Avenue. I suddenly caught sight of something in the road. I bolted from the car, leaving the motor on, my pace slowing the closer I got to the debris that had grabbed my attention. There I stood before the flattened corpse of an animal. I slowly knelt to see if it was Tamino.

Crouched near the remains of a cat with his coloring, I heard myself delivering the news to Miss Frantz. But then inches away from the roadkill, I suddenly noticed a tail; Tamino, a Manx, had no tail! Immediately disgusted by the sight before me, I ran to my car and went off for a raucous evening. Tamino stayed out later than I did that night, returning in the morning pretty bruised from his night out on the tiles. From then on, though, I never let that cat out, swapping the garden for a litter box.

The summer ended well, and on the day Alison was due home I was expected at Janet's for supper. She called a few hours earlier to tell me that an administrator at Merwick, the local long-term care facility, had just phoned to say that a room had become available for Ham the next day. Thus my last supper at 4 Orchard Circle was to be his as well. She was rattled, the complexities of her relationship with Ham having given way to the recognition of an impending seismic shift, but she still wanted to go ahead with my visit that evening. I would bring supper, I insisted. With a sigh of relief, she also told me that I was to have a drink with Alison before coming round for a meal.

As though choreographed, Miss Frantz arrived home shortly thereafter. No longer the fearsome academic who had departed, she immediately presented herself as a wry, dry, and subversive character, clearly brought up to speed on my tenancy by her dutiful sister. Tamino had survived, and it was a good thing that cat could not fill her in about having been under house arrest.

I helped her make gin and tonics—"Don't spare the horses," she growled.

Nibbles were quickly produced, and we went to the garden room to catch up. When it was time for a second drink, we both returned to the kitchen, where she insisted that we have some pickled beets. In the course of shifting them from a plastic container to a fiddly china bowl, she dropped some on her feet. I grabbed a sponge and started wiping the maroon liquid off her toes. Gales of laughter ensued, and our friendship was sealed.

"You must call me Alison," she ordered.

After downing that second drink, I excused myself, explaining that I was responsible for supper at Janet's that evening. She begged off, confessing her exhaustion from jet lag as I left.

Arms laden with pizza boxes, I had trouble ringing the bell and simultaneously letting myself in, as had become the custom. Ham was in a chair near the big window in the living room, appearing to read the newspaper. He waved me through to Janet, who was out on the terrace. Upon hearing me, she put down a flower pot and opened her arms wide to hug me, but was thwarted by the warm boxes.

She brightened at the mystery of the supper I had brought, girlishly squealing, "What's all this?"

I remembered Janet mentioning that she had never tasted pizza. She pronounced it exactly the way it was spelled.

"It's pizz-uh," I announced.

I had learned early on, after trying to correct her pronunciation on occasions, that saying things her way demonstrated respect for her take on the world. When I gingerly pointed out such quirks, she would relate them to her years at Smith College, the logic of which always escaped me.

The pizzas, placed on elegant Georgian silver trays between candlesticks, became the centerpiece of an evening filled with laughter and reminiscence, allowing us odd pleasure during "the last supper"; amidst the merriment, Ham turned and thanked me, calling me Peter for the very first time. At the door, as I was about to depart at 9:15 pm, Janet asked me to accompany her with Ham to Merwick the next morning before my own departure. I agreed but grew uneasy about the role I was playing in this last stage of Ham's life. If only he had not called me Peter.

INSTANT MESSAGING

A notice appeared on the bulletin board in Princeton's Jones Hall inviting students who could speak Chinese to interview with J. P. Morgan. In the early 1970s, only Ping-Pong diplomacy offered a connection between China and America; the notion of being prepared for careers in trade was hardly the path planned for academic sinologists. Still, this rare opportunity for a glimpse into the financial world, offered by the ultimate white-shoe firm, heightened our professors' curiosity, and they encouraged us to sign up for interviews.

During an early spring snowstorm, I trudged across campus to my appointment wearing galoshes and a makeshift outfit, the best I could do as a graduate student. My lack of style was seemingly trumped by my ability to speak Chinese, because the recruiter asked if I could visit corporate headquarters on Wall Street in New York at my convenience. I was told to expect a call shortly to set something up.

About a week later, a man named Neville Fletcher III extended a most gracious invitation. "Might you be coming up to the city soon?" he inquired.

"As a matter of fact, I plan to be there in about ten days, for Passover," I replied.

We agreed to meet on the Friday of that week. He impressed me with his personal warmth, and by extension that of his firm—an institution that had previously seemed daunting, as reflected by Mr. Morgan's nasty nose on his iconic photograph.

When the time came for my interview, luck was with me. I found a parking spot right near J. P. Morgan, and after looking for bullet holes in the facade—souvenirs of an anarchist's assassination attempt on the legendary financier—I entered the limestone building.

My recollection of that meeting is blurred, not by the passage of time but because of the uniformity of those I met. No one was bald; all laughter was hearty; and everyone seemed to have been dressed by the same haberdasher. Looking back, I reckon that my brown suit and blue shirt—and my D. H. Lawrence beard—made quite an impression on them as well. In any case, after a full day of discussions about China I left feeling valued.

On my way back to Princeton, I turned the radio up, singing Motown at the top of my lungs as I cruised along the New Jersey Turnpike. I was buoyed by my Wall Street experience—and the prospect of the Mrs. Dalloway party I was to attend that night.

Back at the Lawrence Apartments, I stopped at the mailbox in the entry hall and retrieved a letter addressed to me, then went upstairs to open it. The stationery was thick and finely engraved. On it, Neville Fletcher III had written that, after careful consideration of my qualifications, J. P. Morgan was unable to offer me a position. I stood there baffled by the enormous gaffe I must have committed that day—and how the letter could have beaten me home.

As I recounted my bewilderment to friends that evening, all was revealed when one of them asked, "Why didn't you just say Easter?"

REVENGE AT THE A-KITCHEN

Waldo, my pal from DC, looked like he was right out of a Scott Fitzgerald novel, with slicked-back blond hair parted down the middle, preppy glasses, and crisp chinos. A quirky and subversive guy who could fall asleep in his wing tips, Waldo was a literal fellow who spoke by rounding his mouth to produce sounds that came from the very back of his throat. His simultaneous projection of rectitude and whimsy made him irresistible as a friend. Waldo took pleasure in my obsession with China; in front of others, he encouraged me to show off in Chinese. His advocacy touched me.

Waldo's family, though passing for a pillar of the community in the leafiest of Pittsburgh suburbs, was full of contrasts and drama. His mother was a nurse; his father a Christian Scientist; and his twin brother, who had married a black woman, had been drummed out of the corps. Waldo had lost his younger sister in a car crash.

Waldo often came to New York for visits, and over time informally adopted my family as his own. While my clan had its share of turbulence, there was acceptance in our house that delighted him. My mother had a knack for gathering people together at parties. I never quite knew if she left the guest list to chance or gave it great thought. There was Beata, a friend my mother had met at Hillside Hospital, where both were being treated for nervous breakdowns. She had the thickest of

German accents and the sharpest of profiles. During the war, she had shared her mother's Long Island home with English musicians Benjamin Britten and Peter Pears. Selma, another regular, had started out as my mother's colleague. Once married to a White Russian naval officer, she had taken two Chihuahuas in her brassiere to the movies and had witnessed a murder that put her on a gangster's payroll for life. Others in attendance were Dave Krause, who had been best man at three of my father's four weddings; Dave Kaplan, an old suitor who wrote for the *Daily News*; my cousin Jay, an actor and singer; and Aunt Marcy. They were all part of my domestic landscape. For Waldo, this was a place as far from home as he could get.

Along the way, Waldo met Jasmine, the elegant and fetching daughter of a Pakistani diplomat posted to Washington. She quickly became a charming addition to our set. Yet eventually Waldo withdrew from our friendship.

Well after things had gone quiet, I became seriously ill with pneumonia and was confined to McCosh Infirmary at Princeton. At last, I was permitted to return to my apartment overlooking the golf course, which I shared with Ned, an English major with a resonant voice, a mop of curls, and a sweater covered with reindeer. Known as "RDB"—Reindeer Boy—Ned had the living room, where he slept with an enormous fan perched on the sill to provide white noise. Always taking pains to record the most mundane matters in his desk diary, one day he jotted down, "Two loads—laundry," which I noticed with incredulous amusement. To this day, I call him "Two Loads."

Immediately after I entered the empty apartment the phone rang, and I was happy to hear Waldo's voice. He had not known that I was sick, and when I told him, he immediately announced that he and Jasmine would drive right up to see me.

He asked that I book them a room at the Nassau Inn and said he would give me a call as soon as he arrived in Princeton, adding, "And by the way, Jasmine will want to go back to that terrific Chinese restaurant in the gas station where we've been before."

When I suddenly recalled that my doctor's only discharge instruction from the infirmary had been not to venture out in the night air, I commented, "My mother came down and stocked the house so I could stay close to home for a few days. The doctor warned against going out in the night air. I'll just pop a roast in the oven and invite some folks over. I would enjoy the company, and I'd like you two to meet some special people."

Sounding more like Hal in *2001* than sweet Waldo, he simply repeated Jasmine's desire to go back to the A-Kitchen. Considering the combination of the cuisine and special treatment they gave me, it was no surprise that she had fond memories of the place.

A few hours later Waldo called from the Nassau Inn. I suggested that we meet at Prospect, an architectural oddity that had once been the president's house but was now the faculty club. "Its gardens on such a spring day would be perfect,"

I said. "We'll have a bit of time to stroll before everyone shows up for roast beef."

I was hoping the aroma of the meat in the oven was seeping through the receiver, obliterating Jasmine's desire for Chinese food. There was silence.

Waldo, Jasmine, and I met in that glorious garden, overlooked by the newly constructed glass dining room that jutted out from the back of the building. After hugs and requisite exchanges, I gingerly reiterated my thoughts for the evening meal at home, but Jasmine could not be dissuaded. So rather than risk a scene, I agreed to switch venues, insisting, though, that we go at an early hour.

Cutting short our walk, we parted. I returned home, turned off the oven, made a reservation at the A-Kitchen, and called my friends to alert them to the change of plans.

Arriving at the restaurant before the others, I was welcomed warmly by the owner. I made him promise that he would speak only to me and not utter one word in English to my party during the course of the evening. The others soon arrived, delighted to see me out of the infirmary. Jasmine was particularly charming, and I found her performance all the more objectionable in light of her willful intransigence.

The Pakistani diplomat's daughter enjoyed a pork banquet that evening, much to my furtive delight. I kept that secret until Waldo and Ann, his new bride, showed up to stay with me in Beijing on their honeymoon many years later.

PASSPORT

My father asked me what I wanted as a gift for finally getting my PhD. I don't know what came over me, but I didn't agonize.

"Passage on the QE Two," I blurted out.

He peered back quizzically through his aviator glasses, unused to such directness, and simply agreed. I was finally thrilled by my father.

Later that day, he called, prepared to chat about the trip's details. It was most unlike him to swiftly follow up on something with such commitment. I grew suspicious

"By the way, Monna and I would be delighted to spend time with you on your adventure. We'll be tagging along," he confessed.

I now knew the price I was to pay for the trip. I said nothing. I had run out of courage and still really wanted to go.

The plan was to meet at JFK on Memorial Day, fly off to London, and sail back. During one of our discussions, he let it be known that this trip was not his idea of a good time but that he was deferring to me in light of my achievement. It turned out that my travel request had been a perfect fit for Monna's agenda, with her brand of overdrive now informing my father's waning interest in the excursion. While thinking I had been an appreciated majority of one, I now realized that I was again a pawn in the never-ending games played out between my father and his wealthy fourth wife.

On the Saturday immediately prior to our scheduled departure, a friend from the bank's training program who had moved to California dropped by for a visit. That Mills had made the effort obliged me to rein in my excitement about the trip since I was determined to pay him the courteous attention he deserved. I asked if he'd like some iced coffee. It was a mighty hot day, and I was sure it would taste good to both of us. My secret was making the cubes out of coffee as well, so as not to dilute the flavor.

As I reentered the living room and placed his drink on the table before him, he held out my passport and queried nonchalantly, "Do you know this has expired?"

I went about my business as a host, as though paying no attention would make the words evaporate. Then he shoved the passport in front of me, his finger pointing at the dates. It had expired in March. As if on automatic pilot, I then stood on the sofa and began taking pictures off the wall, setting them down and regarding them as though considering their rearrangement. Mills obviously recognized my panic and sat me back down. The prospect of telling my father that he would be going off on a trip that he never really wanted to take with only his wife filled me with dread.

"Call the airline and see what they have to say," Mills advised, his voice calm.

I dug out my Pan Am ticket and looked for a number. I called only to hear a recording. Since this was Memorial Day weekend, I was referred to a special number. I dialed again, and a man answered. I launched into my tale, which must have been incomprehensible because he gently interrupted me, giving assurances that he was accustomed to emergencies and would try to help. He claimed there was a number at the passport office for just such situations, but I would only prevail in my request if I gave a convincing account of a desperate situation. Pivotal to my success was not telling the authorities that I already had a ticket. Instead, he advised me to say I had an emergency requiring a sudden trip to London that had caused me to notice that my passport had expired. He coached me to calm down, get my story straight, and then take my chances. His kindly counsel made me feel so good that I thought I had already solved the problem.

Mills helped me prepare for my call to the passport office. I managed to weave fact with fiction, as though just enough bits of truth would hold the story together that I was about to recount. There had to be some urgency in my voice since my tale hinged on a mishap involving my father. Actually, panic came from the peril awaiting me if I did not succeed.

Squeezing Mills's hand, I sat quietly then dialed the number. An image came to mind of a skeptical group of Foreign Service officers on a speaker phone prepared to wet themselves laughing at yet another outlandish tale of woe whined down the wire.

"I need your guidance and would not have called unless this was really serious," I intoned.

"I'm listening," the clerk flatly replied.

"My father, who had open heart surgery, was finally well enough to make a trip to London. But it looks like he traveled too soon. He's stranded there with my stepmother, who is in no shape to sort out his care."

The lies were now coming thick and fast. He pointedly interrupted, though, asking specific questions, most of which I answered truthfully.

"Who is your father's cardiologist in America?"

"Dr. Gench," I seamlessly replied. How could I ever forget the cigar-chomping surgeon in a hospital room filled with oxygen canisters?

"How long has your father been married to your step-mother?"

"Sixteen years," I stated, after a nanosecond of math. Adding a personal touch to enhance my credibility, I explained, "She lost her first husband suddenly, which makes this all the tougher for her." It was actually her youthful second husband who had indeed died of an asthma attack.

"Where are they staying in London?" he continued at a good clip.

"The Connaught," I volunteered, the perfection of this whopper only compromised by my placing emphasis on the wrong syllable of the landmark hotel's name.

After a few more exchanges, the inquisition was over. He expressed genuine concern and gave me instructions on how to obtain an emergency passport. I was told to purchase a ticket to London—he advised me that only Air India was open today—and then report to an unmarked bronze door at Rockefeller Center on the floor of the passport office, which was open twenty-four hours a day. He gave me very detailed instructions, more suited to Hernando's Hideaway than a place to arrange for a document.

By now, I already should have been bound for Forest Hills to see my mother before going off on my trip. I called her to make casual mention of a delay. I knew I had to hang up swiftly or her remote X-ray capabilities would enable her to discern a hoax.

Mills and I parted downstairs. I was grateful that he had made the discovery in advance of my showing up at the airport and had stuck around to help me out as well. He had also been privy to my mad performance, with which he could entertain diners for a long while—and he did, I gather.

Off I then went to the Air India office. Although I knew I would be cashing in the ticket immediately after obtaining a new passport, the outlay of such a large sum of money heightened my anxiety. After all, I was only an entry-level bank trainee. The Indian clerk was on his own, and he lifelessly tended to my request. Recently, in one of the bank's training sessions, we had been given an Indian case study involving letter of credit documents that had been eaten by a cow and asked to opine on the appropriate action to be taken. Fighting my inclination to start telling the fellow about the case, I managed to suppress the urge to giggle.

With ticket in hand, I dashed over to Rockefeller Center expecting to come upon a lone unmarked bronze door near the passport office, but all were bronze and unmarked. Finally, one was opened by a gracious official who was sympathetic to my family emergency. After giving him my new airline ticket, he swiftly went about his business. He then ushered me over to an alcove, where he photographed me. It seemed to take less time to get my new passport than to get the ticket. To be sure, its immediate return was going to be a dismal chore. Once back at the Air India office, I could afford to be patient. It was only then that I took a look at my new passport photo and noticed I looked like Jack Nicholson in *The Shining*.

I was soon bound for Forest Hills on the E train to visit my ailing mother and Aunt Marcy. En route, I anxiously mulled over the story I was going to serve up as an excuse for my tardiness. As I entered the apartment, both women stared at me, commenting on my ashen complexion. Melting into the sofa with great relief, I fessed up and immediately devoured cookies and comforting coffee-milk.

At the airport, my father did take notice of my new passport. He gave me a penetrating glance, but I ignored it. I have a few vivid memories from that trip: going to see both halves of *Nicholas Nickleby* in the West End on the same day; being bankrupted by my stepmother, who expected me to pay for lunch at The Connaught; and seeing the Statue of Liberty early in the morning as we entered New York Harbor.

Empowered by my adventure, I returned to the apartment on West 56th Street, where my mother was staying in my absence, having enjoyed being back in the city during a period of comparative well-being. After chronicling my adventure, we turned to the arrangements for the garden party following my Princeton graduation. With lots of people coming from far and wide, there was much to be done. Very high on my horse, I rode roughshod over her, taking exception with some of her suggestions and plans that had already been made.

She simply turned to me and said, in the silkiest of tones, "Passport." Forever after, her mere mention of that word had the power to demote me back to childhood.

UNINTENDED
CONSEQUENCES

I don't know exactly how Barbara, a fellow sinologist at Princeton, found her passion in life, but she did—and it stuck. She wafted about the East Asian studies department, a petite figure, dressed in layers of caftans, shawls, and ponchos, very much out there with the fairies. Although Song poetry was her avowed field of expertise, it was Chinese cooking that finally swept her away.

I recall being invited to her dorm room for supper. Expecting predictable student fare of pizza or macaroni and cheese, I was confused when no food was in evidence. We sat on the floor on opposite sides of a trunk, which had been tastefully covered with a blue and white cotton Japanese textile, upon which were fiddly little white bowls. Suddenly, Barbara got busy; from drawers in desks and boxes under the bed, a feast of varied marinated delicacies and rice magically appeared. I was as much in awe of her resourcefulness as her culinary ability, leaving the room impressed but still hungry.

We saw a lot of each other that summer. Barbara coped with general exam pressures by maniacally diving into the town pool. I handled things differently, tanning myself in a Speedo, swimming laps, and trying very hard to appear fetching. Barbara ultimately gave up academia and moved to California, leaving Song poetry to others. After her trail had gone cold for some time, anecdotes started to trickle back from the West Coast attesting to her growing reputation as a Chinese cook. There was talk of a newspaper column, a restaurant, and even a liaison with Danny Kaye, a maven of Chinese cuisine as well as comedy.

I was then hired to teach by a fine Jesuit school in California—the University of Santa Clara—located in the environs of San Francisco. In advance of my departure, my mother hosted a farewell party for me at the Russian Tea Room, the magical watering hole "slightly to the left of Carnegie Hall," where she had once sat next to Picasso. To assure a smooth landing, my friend David, an art historian at Princeton who hailed from Palo Alto, kindly alerted his parents to my arrival on the West Coast.

His mother, a charming Southern lady, called after I was well settled to tell me that David would be paying a visit, mentioning off-hand that he also wanted to get together with another Princetonian in the Bay Area. I'd have to wait for the details, though, until he got home. I was also, of course, expected for Sunday lunch. Later that week David called to fill me in on his schedule, adding that we really should make an effort to call on Barbara, who, he assumed, was languishing in San Francisco. He offered to make the arrangements, suggesting that once we had finished Sunday lunch with his family, we go to town and have supper with her.

After enjoying a jolly afternoon with his family, we took leave for our appointment. David mentioned that Barbara had been thrilled to hear from him, promising to take us to the best restaurant in Chinatown. Surprisingly, she was living in Pacific Heights, a rather grand neighborhood for our bohemian pal. While we were allegedly rescuing her from loneliness, we could not help but comment that she had, indeed, landed on her feet. I knew the area, though my own familiarity with it was accidental. On my first visit to the town's Opera House, where I'd had a standing-room ticket to hear *Don Giovanni,* it was my good fortune to meet a dowager named Elly Offen. During intermission, in my drip-dry Haspel suit I fortuitously jostled her while in line to get a drink in the bar. Though our chat was brief, an elaborately lettered invitation soon arrived at my apartment, and I quickly became a regular at her salon. It was usually filled with painters, writers, and mysterious folks—all of us immensely enjoying her warm hospitality. An Austrian émigré who fled during the war, she had lived in this neighborhood for decades, which Barbara was now coincidentally sharing.

David and I finally located Barbara's number, which was painted just inside an alley. We passed through a dark tunnel, only to emerge into the glory of an English garden. Barbara spotted us from the open porch, welcoming us effusively and immediately explaining that while she could not have dinner with us, the balance of the afternoon was ours. But the phone kept ringing; and each time she returned to us our afternoon together was cut shorter. Offering us fresh pear juice, she went into the kitchen and prepared it noisily, with one hand on a blender and the other on the phone. Then, as she served the stuff in fragile stemware we were told that our visit was about to end, leaving David and me bewildered.

"Can you do me a favor, though?" she pleaded. "I need some help getting my stuff to the laundry."

The viscous pear juice was not for chugging, so much of it was left in the glasses as we were hurried out into the street. Each of us was now clutching an enormous bag of laundry and trudging up and down the hills of Pacific Heights. After covering current Princeton gossip and wondering how much farther we would be walking, I casually asked her why she had waited so long to do her wash.

In a sweet, disembodied voice, she replied, "I have crabs, so I had to strip the beds and do all the towels."

Then she seamlessly began making polite inquiry about Chinese eateries near the University of Santa Clara.

David froze, the laundry bag he had been holding immediately falling to the pavement. It took me a bit longer to react as I marveled at Barbara's delivery of the news. The rest of our walk was a lot slower, two of the three bags now being dragged along the street until we arrived at our destination. Barbara was keen to get on with her appointed rounds, and we were eager to distance ourselves from the laundry. Making strained good-byes, we swiftly left her, but my encounter with Barbara and her crabs did not keep me from Pacific Heights. Elly's soirees continued to delight.

My next visit to Elly's home coincided with the announcement of the verdict in the trial of Dan White, the man accused of murdering Mayor George Moscone and Supervisor Harvey Milk, the latter being the first openly gay public official in America. White, a disaffected and unstable politician, got off easy, his lawyer's strategy predicated upon a newly devised defense called diminished capacity—a dicey strategy dubbed the "Twinkie Defense," which hinged on the notion that an overload of sugar had triggered a temporary loss of reason on the part of the defendant. As I drove to Pacific Heights listening to the car radio, a bulletin interrupted the music, announcing that a boisterous demonstration protesting the verdict was underway in the Castro. While singing "All of Me" along with Willy Nelson, I maneuvered my beat-up station wagon to avoid the disturbance, finally arriving at Elly's. News of the demonstration had already set the tone for the evening, with people irate about the verdict, in full sympathy with those out on the barricades. Depressed by the outcome of the trial as well, I could not help but marvel that well-intentioned people had crafted a defense whose first beneficiary was the killer of a Democratic mayor and a gay supervisor. Sipping a drink amongst the great and the good at Elly's, I casually opined that sometimes laws we like work for people we don't like. Then, in a flash, a journalist lunged and tried to hit me.

That failed punch contributed to the ease with which I was able to leave California, a place of murder and intolerance. For Barbara it was different. She went on to flourish in

San Francisco, opening a subsequently renowned restaurant called China Moon. Sadly, though, she died of cancer at age fifty-three.

THE LAST STRAW

*M*y interview at the annual Asian Studies jobs bourse had gone well, although I lost my cashmere scarf, blown from around my neck and carried aloft by a Chicago gust. The tap dancing I had learned at Oberlin and Middlebury, cited on my curriculum vitae, had not seemed to have done me any harm. In fact, Tim O'Keefe, the history professor who interviewed me from the University of Santa Clara, had gotten a kick out of the detail. He offered me a tenure-track teaching job.

When the time came, my friend Larry volunteered to share the driving with me out to California, which was a good thing since I was fit for the chore only in the early mornings. At the drop of a hat, I was more than willing to check into a motel for a swim well before lunch. Thanks to him, we made it, although his own eccentricities seemed to magnify by the mile. What had started out as a road trip—both Larry and Jack Kerouac had coincidentally set out from Riverdale—ended as a journey with a stranger at my side.

I had not yet finished my dissertation, which was no surprise since the topic was only of interest to my advisor. But once settled in at the University of Santa Clara I labored seriously over my Ming texts, the academic environment lending itself to meaningful progress. By day, I happily taught courses on Asia, my favorite being an introduction to the Chinese classics.

The Confucian Analects had long captivated me, but I felt duty-bound also to introduce the Dao De Jing, a Daoist text of great renown, to my students. At around the same time, there was a movie called *Straw Dogs* that had taken audiences by storm. Hearing about its heavy dose of violence, I gave it a miss as my eyes would have been covered for most of it. But that didn't stop me from mentioning the film early in my lecture on Daoism, its title having come from this very book, read by the director, Sam Peckinpah. Expecting to earn kudos from students by making the connection, I looked around the room only to be greeted by blank stares. I immediately knew that they could not get the link between the film and the classic because they had not read the assignment. Then, like an affronted robot, I gathered up my things and left in silence, well before the end of class.

Such an implosion of temper was unlike me. As I calmed down over some iced coffee in the student center, I realized that I was not only personally offended, but had taken umbrage on behalf of China. I also knew that such a display of intemperate behavior demonstrated that I was no Daoist.

I now had to figure out my reentry when the class next met. Although eager to get it right, I made my way back to class two days later with no plan in mind. Simply appearing in the room, I replayed the *Straw Dogs* introduction as though for the first time, but in this rendition I didn't get very far before my words were greeted by yapping students on their hind legs, keen to comment on the classic and the movie.

At registration the next semester, I was doing my shift at the desk, distracted by some book I was reading, when I became aware of two students standing over me.

I heard one of them say to the other, "Lighte teaches this course. He got pissed off about some dogs and walked right out of class."

RECALLED TO LIFE

I was now back in New York. With my mother terribly ill with heart disease, I was obliged to take responsibility for her medical insurance claims. Though she had recognized her inability to deal with the avalanche of forms, she insisted that she be kept abreast of the process. One evening, her cross-examination unrelenting, I grew too angry even to fight with her. She suddenly took note of my simmering silence.

"I know what you're thinking, Cookie," she sagely commented.

"No way," I snapped back.

"You're wishing I were dead," she volunteered.

She had read my thoughts over the phone, leaving me terrified and ashamed.

"Go right ahead. You do understand that such thoughts in no way inform my health. If you must entertain them to cope with my inquiries that's just fine. Now answer my questions."

My mother was soon in Roosevelt Hospital awaiting surgery. When the day of the operation finally came, I received a phone call well before dawn.

"Do you have any nail polish remover?" a nurse barked. Awakened from a deep sleep, I was befuddled.

"Mrs. Lighte has polish on, and if we can't see her nails, oxygen... blood levels..." she said, her voice trailing off.

"I'll be right over," I replied.

There I soon was, removing Carnelian from my mother's toes and fingers, barely in time for her to be wheeled off to surgery. Left standing alone in the room, not sure if I would ever see her again, I realized how much I had enjoyed doing something for her rather than trying to figure her out. Off I then went to the waiting room, where I later met up with Aunt Marcy and Vivien, a family friend. Monna, my stepmother, happened to be in town and insisted upon dropping in. Aunt Marcy, Vivien, and I knew we were in for a long haul when Monna unfurled a piece of complex French needlepoint that had not one stitch in it.

As the day wore on, blood donors, relatives, and friends dropped by bringing snacks and good cheer, encouraging us to go for little walks along the corridors or outside on Columbus Avenue. When Dr. Yeoh, the surgeon, finally appeared, he told us that the damage caused by my mother's childhood rheumatic fever had complicated the procedure. There had been difficulties restarting her heart. Since she would be on life support for several hours, he encouraged us to take a break and return in the evening. Nobody moved, but I knew that Monna was no longer entitled to be present at so intimate a time.

I casually suggested that she come out with me to get some air, hoping that the lure of either the Morgan Library or Bergdorf's would distract her from the vigil. It worked. She left me and walked eastward along 57th Street—Bergdorf's had won the day. I was not ready to go back to the hospital so I continued on. Cutting through 56th Street past the Parc Vendome, where I had received the dawn call, I then turned south onto 5th Avenue, quickly becoming aware of crowds thickening as I neared St. Patrick's Cathedral. Arriving at the landmark, I saw John Paul II, the skiing Polish poet whose election to the papacy had caused a stir, virtually aglow as he stood in front of the main entrance.

My mother miraculously survived the surgery, which was followed by months of recuperation in the hospital. One morning, while I was in training at my new job, the phone rang at the metal desk shared by novices at Manufacturers Hanover Trust Company's brick building at the foot of Manhattan.

"Your mother is being discharged from the hospital late this afternoon. What plans have you made?" an administrator flatly queried.

As I had no inkling of her sudden discharge, neither rehab nor home help had been arranged. Subsequently, I managed to forestall her eviction from Roosevelt, giving me time to sort out her next destination. With the help of social workers, a vicar, a rabbi, and lawyers, my mother was admitted in a few days to the Burke Rehabilitation Center in Westchester, not too far north of the city by rail. That night at the hospital I assured her that her stay at Burke would be brief—and it was not a halfway house to a nursing home. Anxiety lifting, she was delighted to be moving on and eventually home.

After her relocation, we spoke by phone, and she suggested that I skip visiting her that first weekend, a gift that released me from a grinding routine. As we chatted, her voice sounded chirpy while she recounted a new daily regimen. The autumn leaves, her own clothes, and a lively roommate were contributing to her newfound sense of well-being.

When the next weekend rolled around, I went to Grand Central and caught a train to Burke. While en route, I looked around the passenger car, my eyes coming to rest on the profile of the woman sitting next to me, who seemed familiar. Her quiet voice gave nothing away, so I kept stealing glances. Engaged in deep conversation with her traveling companion, she nonchalantly went about her business of unwrapping a toasted bagel while balancing a huge cup of coffee atop a book in her lap.

At last it hit me: she was Margaret Hamilton—the Wicked Witch of the West from *The Wizard of Oz*, Elvira Gulch off her bicycle, the dark side of Glinda, and Dorothy's nemesis! I vowed to respect her privacy, restraining myself from commenting on recognizing her or about the fright and delight she had given to so many, the winning combination that proved irresistible to children. Then the train lurched, and her scalding coffee spilled into my lap, prompting Miss Hamilton to make my swift acquaintance, offering napkins, apologies, and bagels. Her gestures to make amends gave me the opportunity to finally have a chat.

As I later stood before my mother in the day room

at Burke, I excitedly explained the massive stain on my trousers.

"Just imagine," she commented. "A mere pail of water did in the Wicked Witch, and here you are having been doused with hot coffee by the Wicked Witch herself!"

She opened her arms, beckoned me closer, and said with that wry smile of hers, "Nothing could have kept you away. By the way, did you ever manage to send Judy those Tiffany candlesticks I'd mentioned for her wedding present?"

She was back, and I was ready to answer her question.

THE CLOSING

My journey from Manhattan to a loan closing in North Carolina started well before dawn. An Indian customer based in Singapore was buying a polyester plant down south. Although an international banker does not know much about domestic matters, my involvement was prescribed by his nationality. Not only out of my element businesswise, I was also enabling the production of unnatural fibers for export around the world. Nonetheless, I landed in Charlotte, hopeful that my outfit—an intimidating all-wool double-breasted blue suit and suspenders—would more than compensate for my lack of expertise and enthusiasm.

Met by a Dubliner with the oddest twang in gray suede boots, who locked us out of his car, I demonstrated streetwise skill by jimmying open the lock with a hanger kindly provided by a big-haired lady working at the parking lot tollbooth. Declan was now convinced that I was no panty-waisted city slicker. We then drove directly to plush law offices, where an assembly of locals, Yalies, and Hindus awaited me. Wrangling over the documents took most of the day, but it was what happened after the signing that made the trip memorable.

Two clues alerted me to what was coming. The day before I left New York, our customer asked if I could bring some Indian sweets for a celebration he had planned at the plant after the closing. I gladly agreed. Upon my return home from work that evening, the doorman pointed to a huge carton that had been delivered for me; the next morning I dutifully brought the box along with me on the plane. In Charlotte, during intense legal horse-trading, came the second clue—our client demanded hasty resolution of the proceedings since an inauspicious hour was quickly approaching.

With the paperwork finally dispatched, he then insisted that by 4:00 pm we had to be at the plant, a good seventy-five miles away, for festivities. With Hindu deities watching over us, we made it, after passing through a blur of hamlets with names like Polkton and Peachland. Storage tanks suddenly loomed over trees, and as we approached a clearing we found ourselves in a traffic jam of other celebrants.

The first person I met climbing up some stairs to the gathering was a man named Cecil. He pointed to his wife and asked if women were allowed at this sort of thing. Although I knew nothing of what was to come, I put the couple at ease while falling into step with other invited guests. At the top of the steps a Hindu priest imported from Fayetteville was standing at the door in stocking feet, wearing a leisure suit and greeting us all. Once beyond his unctuous introduction, I found myself in a Hindu shrine! There were garlands of flowers and wafting yards of silk—the kind wound into saris—hanging haphazardly along fake wood-paneled walls, with dishes of coins, paper icons, platters of food, kneeling pillows, and exotic bric-a-brac transporting us to foreign parts.

It seemed the moment to ask our customer which delicacy I had hand-carried from New York. Pointing to trays of pistachio-colored sheet cakes cut up like little brownies, he insisted that I taste a piece. Expecting unbearable sweetness, I was pleasantly surprised by a subtle combination of marzipan and halvah. Then, ushered into the next room, I was back in North Carolina amidst long tables piled high with fried chicken, potato salad, dips, chips, and a bar tended dutifully by Southern ladies. The doorway between the rooms separated two worlds.

I was introduced around simply as "the banker." I smiled a lot, thinking that simply being on the premises constituted the ceremony. Then the priest began herding us down a hall into the factory. At a row of spinning machines, the procession halted, with our customer swiftly removing his shoes and socks. The priest approached him, carrying a silver bowl divided into compartments like an infant's feeding dish. Instead of strained vegetables, pabulum, and applesauce, though, there was vermillion, saffron, and rice. A paste was made and smeared on the machine as a garland of flowers was tossed over a protruding handle. The priest then handed the plant's new owner a platter with a burning candle at its center, which he held up and moved in a circular fashion three times clockwise. Next an underling appeared with a bag of coconuts. Handed one, the owner got down on all fours and smashed it, coir and milk flying in all directions. Everyone present broke into applause. This ritual was repeated five more times until all the principals, including myself, had participated.

When my turn had come, I dutifully squatted in my bare feet and smashed a coconut, my red suspenders flapping about. Neither the Hindus nor the local guests knew what to make of me, their impassive expressions a foil for my own embarrassed delight. Then the black mill workers who were hovering at the edges reacted boisterously to the goings-on. When I got up and composed myself, they surged toward me. Before I knew it, I was being carried aloft into the street, the Hindus staring in disbelief. Delivered to a car, I was soon on my way to the airport. After my adventure, I realized there just might be more to banking than double-entry accounting.

SETTLING IN

After a period of tutelage at the bank's head office, I was sent forth to Beijing in 1982; three years later, as a reward for being a pioneer, I was posted to London. There I looked at many flats, but picked one that puzzled the real estate agent. She had insisted upon showing me one property after another, each an off-white, beam-lit bolt hole with too many pokey rooms, the highlight of which was a power shower in a carpeted bathroom. She had also assumed that when it came to location I would only be interested in posh neighborhoods like Chelsea, South Ken, and Belgravia, which actually meant nothing to me, leaving me ignorant of the rest of London. The guidance of brokers rather than the snobbery of Americans had turned this triangle of neighborhoods into a charmed ghetto.

After the agent finally noticed my lack of enthusiasm for her endless supply of cookie-cutter bijou flats, we finally entered a mews house in the crook formed by its wall abutting the arch to the street. Only a tastefully hidden washer/dryer and a narrow staircase leading up to a one-bedroom flat occupied the ground floor. The bathroom had the dreaded carpeting but no power shower, and the kitchen had a tiny fridge that fit under the counter. A grand lady, about whom I had been briefed, awaited me in the sitting room. She was the daughter-in-law of a publican who owned Searcy's, caterers to the queen. After forty-five years of marriage, the publican and his wife were getting divorced, no longer needing this flat for their pied-à-terre.

My eyes were attracted to three windows, each a different size and at a different level in the wall facing out into the mews, while the morning sun beamed in as if on cue. The windowed wall was hemmed in by leaden gray curtains covered in enormous cabbage roses. When I commented on such splendor for so quirky a wall of windows, the hostess went into great detail about the quality of the fabric, the history of the pattern, and the insulation that would ensure the flat's toastiness in the winter. I blurted out that upon my return to the apartment at 2:00 pm, if the curtains were gone I'd be happy to take it at the asking price.

Once moved in but still surrounded by random cartons, I went to Peter Jones on Sloane Square to buy a radio and a television. The store's slogan, "Never knowingly undersold," seemed credible. After making my purchases, I walked to their warehouse on Mossop Street to pick them up, then I hailed a taxi and was soon home. But after opening the cartons I noticed that neither appliance had a plug—just a bare wire snaking out the back. I immediately repacked the boxes, dragged them downstairs, found a taxi, and returned to the warehouse. I then recounted my discovery and requested a new radio and television—with plugs.

"Why do you need new ones? Just go to the iron

monger and buy two plugs," the attendant advised.

I stared blankly. Aside from not knowing what an iron monger was, I couldn't fathom an appliance being sold with no plug. For a moment I thought I was back in China, where such misunderstandings were part of comical daily life conducted in a foreign language. When our laughter finally replaced mutual puzzlement, I discovered that nothing in England came with a plug and that an iron monger—a hardware store—would be my next port of call.

Having purchased plugs at an iron monger, I discovered that while a plug might be called a plug on both sides of the pond, they didn't look the same. Housed within a white plastic box were varied colored wires and a fuse. Although there was a tiny diagram on the inside of the plug, it was unclear, and I broke into a sweat and then into a rage as I struggled to get things connected. Finally, after blowing some fuses—luckily I had purchased extras—I got the radio to work and listened to a program on Radio 4 devoted to the making of vinegar. The television was next, which I successfully tackled. I was now prepared to face a four-day weekend in an emptied London.

That night I settled in, trying to convince myself that a stint in London was my reward for a job well done in Beijing. That's what Mr. McGillicuddy, the bank's chairman, had told me. I drifted off listening to the "Shipping Report," "Sailing Away," and "God Save the Queen." A lifelong addiction to Radio 4 had commenced.

In the morning, cheered by unseasonable warmth, I went to the King's Road, passing the punks assembled at the Sloane Square end, and was soon surrounded by sauntering Euro-trash. When my *passeggiata* was over, I called in at the Europa deli. Although I had plenty of tuna fish back in my tiny fridge, the family behind the counter drew me there. They were Mandarin-speaking Malaysians, and I felt at home while chatting with them.

Strolling back, I decided to explore a different route home to Lowndes Close. In no time I was lost, forced to retrace my steps. I never even made it back to the deli. Finally, out of good humor and landmarks, I was forced to ask directions of an elderly woman who seemed to resent the notion of a foreigner being lost in her neighborhood.

As I neared the mews, I heard the ring of a burglar alarm, growing louder with each step. Once back inside the house, I realized the alarm was next door, prompting closure of my leaded bedroom window. I then stretched out on the bed and turned on the television, luckily coming upon a *Carry On* comedy, which I enjoyed watching. Only later was I to learn that the iconic series is a virtual rite of passage into English humor. The alarm continued, but it was bearable as long as I giggled at Kenneth Williams and Hattie Jacques. Then the screen suddenly went dark. I began pushing buttons, fiddling with the outlet, tightening the plug to the set's wire—to no avail. As my frustration with the set increased, the alarm seemed to grow maddeningly louder.

I set out on a long walk to escape the din, fortuitously encountering a policeman. Assuming he was in the area to address the rogue alarm, I expressed gratitude for his attention to the nuisance that he had not even noticed. When I showed impatience with the situation, he told me that he was powerless to halt the bell, ticking off various legal statutes justifying his paralysis.

I walked on, noting my route in order to find my way back. After finally running out of wanderlust, I tentatively returned to the environs of the mews hoping to hear no alarm, but I had no such luck.

Back upstairs that evening I abandoned my bedroom, which was closest to the alarm, took a blanket and the radio and camped out in the sitting room. I was torn: on the one hand, I wanted to use the earplugs given to me on the plane from Beijing to block out the sound, while on the other hand I wanted to listen to the radio. After much thrashing about on the sofa, which was too short for me, I worked out an arrangement with the radio up against a plugged ear and finally fell asleep.

The alarm was still sounding at dawn, but I took heart in knowing that my pal Seth would be arriving that day—my first visitor to London. I allowed him only the briefest of turn-arounds—a shower and some coffee—before we left the flat, my desire to escape the bell greater than my obligations as a host. But upon our late return to the house the alarm was still ringing. The bedroom was abandoned by both of us. Seth instantaneously succumbed to jet lag on the sofa where I had slept the night before as I struggled to re-create my earplug-radio arrangement on the floor.

The next morning I was eager to go to work, leaving frustration behind. Seth was up as I prepared to walk to the Sloane Square tube station, bound for Mansion House in the City. As I was leaving, he asked if he could help out with chores and errands during the day before we met up in the West End to go to theater that evening.

"Please return the television for me and tell them it just doesn't work. And make sure you get the plug back," I requested.

By the time we got home from the theater, the alarm had stopped, and a new television was working.

A year later the prospect of bank holidays no longer left me with a sense of dread. I could now find Lowndes Close, bicycle around town with ease, and visit the West Country on weekends, but I was always aware of the fact that there was no point in trying to go native. It was better to be a self-aware foreigner than a deluded one, even though I was well stuck into *The Archers*.

One balmy Saturday afternoon, while stretched out after a long bike ride up to Highgate, I was watching *Brief Encounter* when the screen suddenly went dark. The memory of that first long weekend immediately came back. Now, in the absence of an alarm, I noticed a loud click accompanying the failure of the television. I checked the outlets, which had little switches on them controlling the current, and the knobs of the TV itself. Then I spied a quaint brass device to the right of the bed at eye level. After studying what appeared to be a derelict thermostat, its tarnished surface mysteriously calibrated with faint lines, I tried to move the pointer along the gauge. As it barely shifted, the television came back on. I realized that the sudden rise in temperature must have tripped the thermostat, which had mysteriously turned off the television. Thinking back, I realized it had been warm the year before when the very same thing had happened.

But this year was different. I laughed as I surrendered to a television set that was controlled by the weather.

HELMUT AND THE TURKEY

*J*ust as I immediately hang pictures on the wall to put down roots when I move into a new place, I decided to host Thanksgiving dinner in my new London flat after arriving from Beijing. The turkey was key, its importance heightened not only by my sojourn in distant China but by the fact that my grandfather had been in the poultry business. There would be no Butterball on my table! I was going to Harrods for an organic bird.

At Harrods, the Food Halls could have been a jewelry store so extraordinary was the quality, style, and opulence of its produce. It took me a while to find the fowl and poultry counters in the vast space, and even after I had, I quickly learned that talking to a pheasant chap about a gobbler just wouldn't do. I finally found the right gentleman, who seemed to enjoy dealing with Yanks and was au fait as well, with all the fixings. He also proudly announced that he and his wife had recently returned from "Hooston," trying to put me at ease, unlike so many of his compatriots who often opted for snide asides. I pleasantly acknowledged news of his travels, taking pains to properly pronounce the name of the city. He took no notice.

When finally presented with the bill for my order, despite the near parity between sterling and the dollar the total was shocking, but I had already arranged to have it sent round to my flat. He asked one last time, as I was stepping away from the counter, if I'd be cooking the turkey myself.

"Of course, I already have the recipe for the stuffing," I commented over my shoulder while walking away, knowing that Aunt Marcy had sent it over in a bank pouch that she had secretly used for magazines.

As promised, early on Thanksgiving morning the turkey was delivered, its wrappings so exquisite that it felt more like Christmas. The stuffing was ready for its destination. I checked the cavity because I was not about to make the mistake my cousin had years before while preparing her first turkey, of leaving the plastic bag filled with giblets inside the bird along with the stuffing. That was the year of our only vegetarian Thanksgiving, with the stench finally masked by nauseating amounts of room deodorizer sprayed throughout the house.

With the enormous bird stuffed, I ceremoniously approached the well-heated oven only to discover that it was too small to accommodate the turkey. I quietly set down the enormous pan and left the kitchen. In the sitting room, I put on David Bowie singing "Young American" and began to dance, in too great a panic to confront the situation. Then, danced out, I immediately ruled out hacking the turkey to bits to make it fit in the oven. I also thought about dashing over to the deli run by the Malaysian Chinese to commandeer any turkey they might have, but dismissed the prospect of serving meat meant for a picnic.

Then Helmut the butler came to mind. The dour and crisp Austrian who ran the bank's dining rooms on Princes Street had been oddly welcoming to me upon my arrival in London. He must have sensed that I was intimidated by the certainty and formality of the Brits, observing me worry about using the dessert spoon atop the plate for soup or passing the port in the wrong direction. He looked after me, and by watching Helmut's eyes I began to learn the rules.

Despite the early hour, I called the bank, and to my relief Helmut was there. After swearing him to secrecy, I confessed my predicament and asked if he could prevail upon the chef to roast the turkey. He assured me of his ability to help, suggesting that I send the turkey into the City by taxi, letting him know exactly when the bird was on its way. In those days, before mobile phones, the precision of Austrian judgment would ensure that the car would be met. He then explained that when the cooking was done he would dispatch the turkey back by taxi, calling me, in turn, when it left the bank. I asked Helmut not to discuss the matter with Paul, my boss, who would be coming to supper that night. My level of anxiety dropped after I had comically loaded the turkey into the back of a cab. The driver was unflappable; as the bird's journey began, I imagined the driver taking little notice of the large roasting pan in the back as he tromboned on all the way to Princes Street, my stuffed fowl just another captive audience.

Back in the flat I was finally able to tend to other preparations for the event. I had managed to track down some folding turkeys that could be flared open and put them on the table. Aunt Marcy had recently sent me an issue of *People* magazine that featured a shockingly obese man named William Hudson on its cover. I perversely placed him on a book stand between the two paper turkeys.

Helmut's call finally came, well into the afternoon, with my panic mounting by the hour. When the taxi arrived, having been delayed by the driver's difficulty in finding the mews, it was a mere fifteen minutes until my guests were due to show up. The massive turkey was splendidly cooked, its skin browned and looking perfect amidst vegetables and potatoes artfully arranged. The bird went right on the table in front of William Hudson. Shortly, the doorbell rang, and guests streamed in, with Paul and his family amongst the first wave.

Warmly shaking my hand and giving me a generous pat on the back, he leaned over and whispered in my ear, "I'm glad the turkey got here before we did."

When I sought out Helmut back in the office the next day to thank him, I saw him laugh for the very first time—in the best possible taste.

AMBUSH IN BLACKHEATH

When I first arrived in London, early in the Thatcher years, gentlemen in the City were still sporting bowlers and carrying tightly furled brollies, and no tunnel link to Europe yet existed. I began taking notice of double-barreled surnames and posh accents, which had to do with my falling in with an old Etonian whose set was crowded with entitled fops.

In the merchant bank, Adrian was the one who told me early on, "No brown in town." He himself wore those double-breasted suits with pinched waists and vents on either side in the back and unbuttoned-down shirts adorned with fiddly cuff links. Not only did I stick to my guns about buttoned-down broadcloth shirts, but my cuffs remained subversively unbuttoned. Brown suits were thrashed out of me, though, and I do like the way the English mix all types of stripes at once.

Those first days at work were terrifying. Before the firm found me a desk on the floor, I was confined to an empty room. To remind people that I was actually in there, I propped the door open with a wastepaper basket.

Anne, a towering Scottish assistant to one of the bosses, once asked for the bin. When I casually wondered aloud what a bin was and why she needed it, she replied, "Ace for the wanc."

It took extensive inquiry to discover that there was a party for someone going off to run a B and B in the Outer Hebrides. To keep the beverage chilled, a pail was needed to hold ice for the wine.

Before the business day began, a manila folder would show up daily on the table in that lonely room of mine. It was filled with copies of correspondence meant to be read, along with the *Financial Times*. It turned out that Tony, the sadistic South African boss who delighted in making grown men weep, had learned this custom of circulation during his time as PA to Siegmund Warburg, scion of a famous German banking family and founder of S. G. Warburg and Co., a major British merchant bank. Another souvenir of Tony's tutelage under Mr. Warburg was a reverential regard for graphology. While still in Beijing, I had received a breezy telex from him asking some folksy questions and requesting that I simply slip my handwritten answers into an envelope—no need to telex my response. That sheet of paper, I later discovered, ended up on the desk of a Mrs. Cambridge for scrutiny in a graphology institute funded by Mr. Warburg. I got the job.

After my desk was finally ready—hardly an elegant antique partners' desk, like the one displayed in the paneled entrance foyer—I sat with my back to Ai-ling, the first female managing director in the City. Born in South America of Chinese descent, she blinked uncontrollably. I quickly realized that I had to accommodate her sense of the workday. She came to life very late in the afternoon, when she finally began focusing on work. Earlier than that she simply intimidated us with her demonstrations of intelligence, largely imparted by peppering us with random questions designed to demoralize, not teach.

After being humiliated one morning for not knowing enough about asset swaps, I bumped into Adrian, who sensed my distress. He immediately invited me to lunch at Sweetings. As reservations were not accepted, we had to get there early to be seated family-style and enjoy delicious fish in this boisterous charmer of a City landmark. Over Dover sole, he told me of his interest in antiques and furniture restoration, casually mentioning that he worked with a fellow named Rodney. He assured me that if I ever needed help with purchases I should not hesitate to ask for advice. When I unburdened myself about the drama of my morning, he commented that such unpleasant encounters were simply rites of passage that came with the territory, but that it was probably tougher for me since I was a Yank.

During a stroll that weekend past an antique shop on the King's Road, I caught sight of two Victorian wing chairs covered in decaying leather. Their comfort beckoning—such a relief from upright Ming—I inquired about them. Tolerated by the Sloane Ranger in golden hubcap earrings and a Hermes scarf who was manning the place, I had to winkle the price out of her, all the while made to feel more like a nuisance than a customer. Newly arrived from China, I did not yet understand the routine required to traffic with this sort of clerk. To her, I was simply a vulgar American—oversexed, overpaid, and over here! I took my leave.

I find it difficult to ask for help, a malady born of a lifetime of being asked for help, but I liked those chairs. So I called Adrian, alerting him to my find. He made it easy for me, putting Rodney at my disposal as he knew the shop well and could check out the chairs.

After a few days, Adrian reported back that Rodney had felt the chairs to be a really good find. In gratitude, I invited the two to supper later that week.

When they rang the bell at my flat, Rodney was hardly what I had expected. Beet-faced, obese, and turned out in threadbare tweed, he swanned in, laboriously making his way up the twisting and narrow stairs, with Adrian in his wake. Once in the sitting room, he deigned to look about, opining on furnishings and knickknacks, wearing an expression that hinted of there being a dead fish beneath his nose. The inspection over, he and Adrian tittered when I served cheese with drinks, then made patronizing remarks about quaint Americans. While not really understanding their banter, I felt uncomfortable in my own house. Then, at the table Rodney proceeded to drink me out of house and home, with Adrian bizarrely in his thrall. The evening finally over, it was good to see the back of them. Adrian appeared in the bank the next morning, effusive in his gratitude for so lovely an evening, offering Rodney's compliments as well.

As I liked Adrian and knew few people in the office, I apologized on his behalf to myself, thereby continuing on with his acquaintance. There were more lunches at Sweetings and many walks throughout the City, exploring streets with names like Crutched Friars and Old Jewry. He introduced me to the glorious St. Stephen's Waldbrook, with Henry Moore's mushroom-like piece in the middle of the dead white church. I also learned about the special relationship the English had with their first ally, the Portuguese. It turned out that because Adrian's family had long lived near Oporto he was bilingual. He spoke of women but always in the context of friendship. Aside from learning about furniture, I wondered if I was enjoying furtive sport.

On one of our strolls, Adrian proposed, "How about popping out to Blackheath for supper at Rodney's?"

Once I accepted, he added that, by the way, Rodney had come across a chest that might be just the thing for my flat. So, a few days later in the pouring rain—my new Swaine and Adency umbrella already lost in a theater—we were on British Rail, bound for his friend's home a few miles southeast of London.

Considering the condescending once-over that Rodney had given my modest home, I was taken aback by his dreary digs. The place was motel-like, hardly the charmingly dog-eared sanctuary I had expected. But his welcome was warm, and I momentarily felt guilty about the pettiness of my first impression. The wine flowed plentifully, but the plates, almost too hot to handle, arrived from the kitchen bearing portions of stringy and fatty meat, limp vegetables, and disintegrating potatoes. I came to learn that the English cared more about the heat of a plate than what was on it.

Rodney and Adrian were a real tag-team, steering the conversation toward antique furniture and getting more detailed as time passed, becoming oppressive in much the same way that an earnest enologist can ruin a glass of wine.

"Let's have pudding after we look at the chest," suggested Rodney.

I hesitatingly followed my two dinner partners through a warren of dark and cluttered rooms, finally halting before an object covered with a shabby bedspread. Then, with fanfare, Adrian removed it. Rodney and Adrian each sighed audibly, their eyes coming to rest on me.

My father came to mind. A connoisseur of art, he was often obliged to comment on something that he didn't like. His stock remark was always, "The light, the movement. . . ." and then he'd move on.

I made my own innocuous comment about this pedestrian piece of furniture and had hoped to return to the table. But there was simply no easy way out, and they seemed to know that. I continued to emit diplomatic expressions of disinterest, but Rodney and Adrian just became more insistent, finally saying that the very reason I had been invited was my tacit agreement to buy the chest.

Faced with this false statement and being physically

hemmed in, I began to panic and forced myself past the two of them, announcing my departure. I made for the front hall, took my coat off the peg, grabbed my briefcase, and bolted out the door, preferring the pouring rain to another moment in that house, where the evening had turned into *Lord of the Flies.*

Without looking back, I heard them snarl, "You can't go!"

Lost in a maze of terraced brick houses, I finally stopped a car to ask directions to the train station. It was far, I was told, as the driver pointed the way, and there was little likelihood of hailing a taxi in this part of town. I carried on, irate about the inconvenience and feeling menaced by Rodney and Adrian's routine when suddenly I became aware of a car inching up beside me.

"But we haven't had pudding yet," shouted Adrian. On I walked, and the car followed.

"We were having such a lovely evening," he continued. I did not stop.

Then finally he said, "We'll take you to the train." The silent journey ended at the station, where I boarded a train, relieved that Adrian was not coming with me.

The next day at the bank, I knew there would be no more lunches at Sweetings. Nor was a word ever said about my visit to Blackheath or the chest. Further conversations were all about the weather and the injustices of my blinking boss.

THE YELLOW PAGES

During my stint in London, I was seconded to Sydney, and the prospect of a reunion with Tom only added to my excitement. He and I had started work at the bank on the same day—October 15, 1979. Aside from that, all we had in common was Ernie, the man who hired us both. Tom had been with Ernie, a little, intense, charismatic fellow, in the National Guard, where they had shared graveyard duty in Arlington Cemetery; their claim to fame had been laying Congressman Mendel Rivers to rest. Years later, Tom had reconnected with Ernie, who was already making his way in banking. I, on the other hand, had met Ernie in my round of interviews. At the end of our chat, he had leaned toward me and suggested that I circle back later in the afternoon, when all my meetings were over. He was keen to get together again, he said, in an almost conspiratorial fashion. Thrilled by the mystery of his attention in the context of possible employment, I later presented myself, as suggested. He asked me to accompany him somewhere, and I dutifully tagged along, full of curiosity about our destination—which turned out to be a barbershop. He beckoned me to sit beside him as he had the works, chatting through a haircut, shave, and manicure. I got the job, and Tom became my friend.

Tom and I made an odd couple, indeed. He was a hulking

Irish redhead who would invite me to his 3:00 am frat parties at Columbia—he still lived there, though he had long since graduated. I never made it. He had also called me on occasion from a ship-to-shore radio while sailing off the coast of Maine, asking me to make excuses for his absence from the bank. Though not up my street, such high jinks were appealing to this awkward, balding Jewish sinologist fond of delis and musicals, who took vicarious pleasure in living two blocks from Studio 54. Yet during our training period we grew so close that we would playfully introduce one as the other, naughtily confusing colleagues throughout the bank. Then there were our lunchtime ferry journeys to the Statue of Liberty that ensured pleasurable afternoons as we coped with the tedium of training at 4 New York Plaza. It was there, though, at the height of the Iranian hostage crisis, that a check endorsed by the Ayatollah Khomeini came across my desk. Our careers eventually took us both away from New York— Tom to Australia, where he still lives today, and me first to Beijing and then to London and beyond.

I was in Sydney for a whole month, happily staying at the Cebel Town House. Far from the glitzy ghetto of tourist hotels, the Cebel was an imperfect jewel, each room different; it was a favorite spot for touring music and theater people who did not want to throw furniture out the windows. I once saw Bob Dylan in the lobby, and on another occasion as I waited in my tuxedo to be picked up for a formal event, Lauren Bacall approached me, saying in an irresistible snarl,

"Either you're my chauffeur or my date tonight, Honey."

One evening Tom suggested supper at The Yellow Pages, in the neighborhood of the hotel. There was a real buzz in this casual and trendy place, and I was happy to have changed out of my suit, but Tom, of course, was still in uniform—his Brooks Brothers dark gray, striped suit and powder blue shirt with initials placed in the absence of a breast pocket. I knew the outfit well only because I had been with him at Brooks Brothers in New York, where he had badgered the long-suffering Mr. Eric over the placement of the monogram.

We were well seated in the thick of things, Tom having left nothing to chance. Next to us were two older gentlemen who looked as out of place as Tom did; however, with all the activity around us, my awareness of that duo was fleeting.

Several drinks later, we were in the middle of our meal when I noticed a huge cockroach crawling up the wall beyond Tom. Finally catching the eye of the waiter, I discreetly brought the bug to his attention, to which the big, butch Aussie replied, "Oh, I just hate those things."

The critter scurried down the wall onto the floor, where it galloped around the restaurant in full view of the other guests. The diners shrieked and comically bobbed up and down. Then it was at my feet. I grabbed my espadrille and whacked the roach, eliciting a round of applause from relieved guests. I awkwardly bowed, having a good laugh, after which we graciously received drinks of gratitude—compliments of the gents at the next table.

In the morning, I rose early, as I always do no matter what time I've gone to bed or how much I've had to drink. On my way to breakfast, I grabbed *The Australian* that had been left in front of my door. Thumbing through the paper, I come upon a review of The Yellow Pages, which highlighted the brave Yank seated next to the reviewer who had saved his fellow diners from a menacing beast.

THE TENT

One evening back in London, I went to The Tent on Elizabeth Street for supper. It was a charming bistro, despite the snooty maître d'. He tried passing himself off as French, but with those cheekbones he could only have been a Hungarian. My friend Seth was again in town, along with his pal Clark, a Canadian known to us as "Krystle" because of his big hair right out of *Dynasty*. The latter, long a London resident, had made the arrangements. Other disparate acquaintances had joined us.

I was on a well-received roll about Australia when a waiter appeared at my elbow, bearing an enormous platter. As I looked at the snow peas, the waiter asked, "*Mange tout?*" to which I modestly replied that there were too many for me to eat them all.

"Why, sir, I would not expect you to eat all of the vegetables," he gently commented.

"My French is not very good, but didn't you just ask me if I'd eat them all?" I continued in a self-deprecating manner.

"I don't speak French, sir," he blankly responded.

My ignorance of the name used in England for snow peas—*mange tout* (French for "eat all")—and the waiter's ignorance of the fact that he was speaking French paralyzed us in bewildered silence. When we had finally figured it all out, only after I began chuckling did the waiter allow himself to follow suit.

After the meal, as we were discussing the possibility of a walk in Hyde Park our waiter came to the table and poured out the very last glass of white wine for Krystle, and with the final drops out came a cockroach! Aghast along with the rest of us, the waiter scurried to get the maître d', who was already on his way over with the bill. Even mild-mannered Krystle could not disguise his distress as he recounted the arrival of the bug in his glass to the aloof Hungarian. Relieved that the matter was now between a guest and the maître d', the waiter joined us in looking to his boss for justice. But the bill was simply proffered to Krystle as it was, with the explanation that since the roach had only been in the last glass, no gesture was necessary.

Scams in old movies came to mind, when beautiful people were caught out with no money at posh restaurants. Whether it was a handy bug or glass shard that would find its way into a late course, if one had just the right whiff of hauteur about him, the maître d' could even be made to bow and scrape as he tore up the bill. This was no film, though. We paid up, slipped the waiter a tip, and never returned.

TWO BRYDGES PLACE

When my friend Edward and I went on holiday to Florence, we happened to meet Henrietta Garnett, author and granddaughter of Duncan Grant. Upon our return to London, we found a gracious invitation from her to a book launch.

As Edward was off on a painting trip to the Quantocks, I went to Henrietta's party by myself. The problem was finding the place. Even with an *A-Z* in hand, I simply could not get to Two Brydges Place. I finally spotted some folks who seemed to disappear into a chink in the wall on the south side of the Coliseum and followed them. The sight of rubbish, dog feces, and derelicts did not bode well. Eventually, though, I spied a brass plate on a door with the right address and rang the bell in relief.

Once inside, I encountered stairs so steep they appeared to be a wall. I made my way up the rickety pile but could not enter the two crowded rooms at the top, so I kept climbing, this time up an even more treacherous flight that wound to a halt in a bit of a space. Happily grabbing a drink from a passing waiter, I navigated toward a window, seeking relief from the smoke and crush of strangers. I was finally able to take a good look around.

The dark walls were covered by a random collection of paintings. There were two rooms on this floor, with people flowing between them. I was almost within earshot of a gangly white-haired older gentleman. His disheveled get-up revealed his status well before I could make out his posh twang. Being very tall, I often end up talking to other tall people at big parties because I can hear them without stooping. Although the din conspired against easy conversation, the man managed to introduce himself as Nigel Nicolson, humbling me no end. His book *Portrait of a Marriage* had been iconic for me. Back at Princeton I had become happily involved with my last girlfriend (I think I was her last boyfriend as well), a member of the Freud clan. Trying to prevail despite being sexually mismatched, we had lighted on this book. It was based on letters found by Nicolson in Sissinghurst Tower—the gardened garret of his mother Vita Sackville West—written to and received from his father, Harold Nicolson. We figured that if Harold and Vita could make a go of things, maybe we could, too. Though my romance with Ellen had long faded, the power of that book had not, and to be in the company of its author was thrilling.

In the course of our lofty chat that evening—literally above the heads of those around us—I asked about his current literary project.

"My son and I are somewhat estranged, and we have contrived a reconciliation. We will be traveling to opposite ends of America, writing letters to each other and meeting up somewhere in the middle of the country," he said.

"Why not simply take him out to lunch?" I quipped.

His blank expression puzzled me.

Trying to recover, I asked, "Where will be your first port of call, Mr. Nicolson?"

"Florida," he replied.

His answer was a gift. I told him of my birth there and described the Miami of my childhood: segregation in pre-Castro days, singing "Dixie" at school instead of the "Star-Spangled Banner," and celebrating the birth of Jefferson Davis rather than that of Abraham Lincoln. "And my father still lives there. In advance of your trip, you might want to get in touch with him," I suggested, as though I were closer to my father than Mr. Nicolson's son was to him.

Mr. Nicolson took down my father's details, confessing his pleasure at the openness of Americans, which, he said, always came as a surprise to him. Maybe America was just the place for emotional cripples to patch things up, I thought, benighted about my own predicament.

My father soon called to tell me that Mr. Nicolson had contacted him. Not only had they chatted at length, but the Englishman had accepted an invitation to stay. Mr. Nicolson confirmed the arrangement just as he was about to leave for America to put things right with his son.

"By the way, you must join that little club where we met. I'll have a word," offered Mr. Nicolson.

And I did swiftly, enjoying his kind sponsorship. To fulfill my membership obligation, I presented Two Brydges Place with *Acquiescence*, a painting based on an I Ching hexagram.

Several months later, a package arrived containing a book of correspondence between Nigel and Adam Nicolson called *Two Roads to Dodge City*, whose first chapter was devoted to the former's time spent on San Marco Island with my father and his wife.

I reflected on how my father and I should have taken a leaf out of the Nicolsons' book to get things right—or maybe I should have just taken him out to lunch.

BASHERT

After I began working at the bank in New York, a kindred spirit suggested that we go for a drink on East 58th Street to a place called Regents East—a long, thin venue with a bar in front and a piano in the back. It was packed with gentlemen in suits, all just having come from their offices. (It was also known as Rejects East, I later discovered.) I quickly made my way toward the music. A late night was simply out of the question, however, since the next morning I had to attend a very early lecture by a member of the bank's senior management team.

I did make it to 350 Park Avenue on time, my steps there rhythmically accelerated by Donna Summer singing "Dim All the Lights" on my new Walkman. I settled into the auditorium with my copy of the *New York Times* and then noticed a gentleman approaching the podium. It was none other than a man I had seen the night before at Rejects East who had comically introduced a camp friend he called Doris Godunov to a circle of chaps.

Several years later while posted in Beijing, I properly met this gentleman named Harry when he was calling on the People's Bank. A towering man with a mane of white hair, he personified the internationalist. His business completed, he chose to stay on a few days to sightsee. One dusty April afternoon in the Forbidden City, we were sipping tea amidst gnarled rocks, potted plants, and flowers. Then we tentatively chatted about our shared lifestyle, and he was most amused about being sighted at the gay watering hole years before. Thereafter, under his courtly wing I was quietly introduced to a homosexual brotherhood of bankers within the firm; the one very much his equal was the formidable John McCarthy, ensconced in a London position that would see him into retirement.

With my tenure in Beijing coming to an end, it was suggested that London might be my next port of call. When I visited England to take a look around, I first met Mr. McCarthy. He welcomed me into an elegant office, the antithesis of the rowdy merchant bank in the building where I might be working. He made an oblique reference to his bond with Harry, alerting me to the fact that cards were already on the table; from there our conversation was about my career, living in London, and his great respect for the chairman. As I was leaving, John suggested that we meet at a pub before going to Sunday lunch that weekend. I asked if I could bring a friend who was visiting from New York. Looking back, John must have mistakenly assumed that Seth—who worked for Air France and had arranged a quick jaunt to London— and I were more than just great pals.

Seth and I turned up at the appointed pub on an unseasonably warm and sunny day. John stood at the bar, the turned-out gentleman at leisure. We enjoyed breezy chitchat over quick drinks, sticking to the niceties of out-of-towners being looked after by the seasoned expatriate. Then we were on our way to a nearby bistro, Le Gourmet, on the King's Road. As we entered, pausing just inside the door, we noticed three waiters at the back of the restaurant. Spotting John, the trio pointed at him and crooned at the top of their lungs, in a move that could have been lifted from a Supremes routine: "Here's Monica!" That squeal instantly stripped John of all affect, and Le Gourmet became a regular Sunday brunch venue once I moved to London in 1985.

It seemed only right, a few years later, to call in at Le Gourmet to tell the aging maître d', Gus, that I had just come from the Royal Marsden, where John lay dying of cancer. He could see that I was shaken and guided me to a table in the back of the empty restaurant. After we raised our glasses to John, I told Gus that I had held a tiny music box close to John's ear and turned the crank. "After the Ball" might have been the last music John ever heard.

I then moved on down the King's Road to the Queens Head, near Sloane Square. While standing in the bar sipping anything but lager— I had never developed a taste for beer, even in my college days—I became aware of a nearby circle of chaps, their laughter sounding too loud for no reason. I noticed a fellow close to me who seemed keen to escape from the bunch. He suddenly pivoted and spoke to me. Rather directly for an Englishman, he asked me what I did.

"I work in a bank," I replied, always uncomfortable with simply saying that I was a banker.

His reaction was as odd as his directness. The usual routine would have been either to glaze over or count the sterling in my pocket.

This fellow, named Julian, continued, saying: "I have to have a think about American bankers. Recently, a director friend of mine was stumped by problems with a new opera. All the experts let him down, but his agent put him in touch with an American banker who calmly got things right for them, and the project quickly moved on. Have you ever heard of *A Night at the Chinese Opera*? I'd like very much to meet an American banker like him!"

Indeed, I had heard of *A Night at the Chinese Opera*. A talent agent named Rich, who was a pint-sized version of Edward Fox, and I had met at a dinner party. We had both shared tasteless giggles after suffering endless stories served up by a fellow whose partner had recently died of AIDS. Though ashamed by our outburst, we had rationalized it by reckoning that the mourner would have been insufferable under any circumstances.

Rich had called me one day, asking for assistance. One of his clients was directing a new opera by a promising composer based on some Chinese materials. There were problems with the veracity of the production, and none of the Oxbridge crowd consulted had been very helpful. Though I was not part of the theater set, Rich was mindful of my passion for matters Chinese and, in desperation, had sought me out. At his request, I then met up with Richard Jones, the director of the new opera, for lunch, and we enjoyed a lively discussion setting the world of Mongol China to rights. Judith Weir's new opera, *A Night at the Chinese Opera*, was going to be just fine.

On the night before the Great Storm of 1987 in the Queens Head, I looked at Julian and said, "You just have."

It was *bashert*—Yiddish for "meant to be." Over a quarter of a century later, we are married, with two daughters and a dog.

MARION LEVY

*M*arion Levy and Duna were quite the pair on the Princeton campus: the imposing sociology professor sported a crown of curly salt-and-pepper hair, a walking stick, a golden rat pin fastened to his collar, and was accompanied by his komondor named Duna, a huge, flatulent, beige Hungarian sheepdog that looked like a giant mop on legs. In class, Duna would sleep below his master's desk in the front of a packed classroom, with Professor Levy holding forth purportedly on modernization in the Far East; but more often than not he'd be jousting with his students, demonstrating the perils of illogic with an uncanny knack for playfully entrapping intrepid souls, or railing against "foreign-language cripples," his term for ill-prepared students of Japanese and Chinese. I marveled at the precision and mirth of Professor Levy's expression. It was no surprise that the East Asian studies department at Princeton had sought him out as its chairman; he was the ideal advocate to go head-to-head with the administration, magically loosening the purse strings.

Years later while I was living in London, Mr. and Mrs. Levy visited England and got in touch, so I invited them home for supper on Oakley Street, down the road from the illuminated Albert Bridge in Chelsea. By now Duna was dead, but Mr. Levy still had his walking stick and golden rat pin. There was much to chat about: their daughter, with whom I had studied Chinese at Middlebury one summer; my thesis advisor, Fritz Mote, who was an object of Mr. Levy's rare admiration; the paintings of Paul Klee, much admired by us all; and the rivalry between Houston and Galveston, Texas—Mr. Levy's hometown.

In a gentle tone, Mr. Levy playfully spoke of his Jewish family. "One day my cousin, the mayor's son, came home from school beaten to a pulp. After being badgered by his father for an explanation, he finally came clean, recounting a bewildering incident. He said a bunch of kids started shouting at him, repeating over and over, '*You* killed Jesus,' and then they jumped him. Once assured that his son was all right, the mayor took the boy by the shoulders, steered him to the door, and said, 'You go right out there and tell those rowdies that it was the Jews in Houston who killed Christ.'"

As the pleasurable evening unfolded, Mr. Levy mentioned a new book he had written called *Our Mother-Tempers*. Its thesis was simple: since mothers pass on values to their children in the first five years of life, men's views of women are, in fact, shaped by women. He was deadpan in observing that the book had gone largely unreviewed— knowing full well, I suspected, that his provocative premise was politically incorrect. Had he stuck to his professional knitting, he certainly would have been given much academic airtime.

"If you ever have some time, Peter," he casually asked, "can

I trouble you to go into some stores to see if the book is available in London?"

The following Saturday I was in the West End on Great Russell Street, calling in at Cornellisen's, a favorite art supply shop where dry pigments were still sold along with nibs and inks. Having made my rounds, I wandered down Charing Cross Road, poking around the bookstores, hoping to track down a tome called *The Great Pavement in Westminster Abbey*.

While I was pausing in front of a well-known feminist bookstore, Mr. Levy's request suddenly came to mind, and I walked in. The shop was staffed by earnest women, and its ambience of worthiness sparked mischief in me. At the till, I made an inquiry about a newly published book written by the American sociologist Marion Levy.

"What's it about?" the clerk casually asked, as if buying time to recall her own knowledge of the title, as a matter of professional pride.

"How women shape children's perceptions," I replied.

As she searched for an order form, I expressed mild surprise that so prominent a feminist bookstore did not stock a title of such import. She genuinely apologized as she took down my details, assuring me of her interest in the book. I started to feel a bit guilty about my ruse but was too far down its path to redeem myself.

When I got home, I wrote Mr. Levy a letter describing my adventure on his behalf; by return post came a copy of his book. The minute penmanship of this grand man's inscription caught my attention:

For Peter Lighte, who did just right.

As ever,

Marion (a well-known radical lesbian writer)

Shortly afterward, I received a call from the bookstore. "The book is in, and by the way, Marion's a man," a voice curtly declared, followed by a loud click.

I was too scared to pick up the book.

REINDEER IN THE GYM

As a young banker in London, I would go for a daily swim at Cannons, a sports center beneath the arches of the Cannon Street Bridge. When Manufacturers Hanover Trust Company moved to the Adelphi Building in the West End, I joined a brand-new gym on Endell Street, a stone's throw from Covent Garden tube station. The clientele could not have been more different from the Cannons crowd. There were actors, media types, students—anyone but City business clones—and I liked it.

One afternoon in the men's changing room, I heard the jangling of metal. I looked up, thinking there might be some sort of glitch in the new ventilation system. Instead, the sound seemed to be coming from elsewhere in the room, where a skinhead covered in tattoos was undressing in front of a locker. Once he was in the buff, all was revealed: a veritable chandelier of metal chains and hooks pierced through and suspended from his bits. So flustered was I by the sight that I burst out laughing. He glowered from afar and then walked straight toward me, his pubic installations not keeping time with his gait. How right Balanchine had been about the impracticality of nude ballet!

Once he had invaded my personal space, I started to babble, inquiring, "Have you ever seen the original film of *Auntie*

Mame—not *Mame*, but the real thing, with Rosalind Russell?"

His metal adornments now still, he stood there regarding me as deeply strange, and I continued on without taking a breath. "During the Depression, Mame lost all her money and was forced to go to work. One of her great pals, Vera Charles, was an actress who luckily managed to get Mame a walk-on part in a Broadway play. Coral Browne, the English wife of Vincent Price, played Vera Charles."

Only then did a glimmer of interest appear in his eyes.

"Mame was hired to be a maid silently bearing a tray of drinks to serve to the guests," I persisted. "Since her arms were encircled in stylish bangle bracelets, a racket preceded her entry, and when she finally moved amongst the crowd she managed to overpower the actors' dialogue with her clacking jewelry before leaving the set. The upstaged Vera was so furious that she hissed at Mame in the wings, 'What the hell have you got back there, reindeer?'"

I began laughing again, less at him than at the invocation of Rosalind Russell, expecting him to join me in the humor of it all. Rather, he simply turned around, his antler leading him away. I slipped out of my colored underwear, into my Speedo, and flung myself into the lap lane, managing to giggle under water.

THE ALBERT HALL

*B*ill, a friend who worked for Amex in Beijing during the early 1980s, asked me to supper with his boss and wife, Teddy and Gudrun, on their grand tour through China. A birdlike man of indeterminate age, Bill had a knack for snaring young men in the lobby of the Beijing Hotel. Despite his compulsive tidiness, he had no qualms about rowdy company up in his room, where every bit of furniture was covered in locally produced blue and white cotton. Happily, I did not fit his bill.

When Gudrun appeared, I thought Ingrid Bergman had entered the restaurant. She wafted over to the table and was as charming as she looked. Teddy seemed happy to bask in his wife's glow. Bill had hinted at his boss's ambivalent sexuality, but the two of them together were actually as camp as a row of tents, bantering throughout supper. As we parted later that evening, Gudrun and Teddy gave me their details, should I ever visit London. Unlike many such offers, I believed them and took them up on the offer when I subsequently relocated there.

They lived in a maisonette at Rutland Gate, high above a large communal garden with a terrace. I was much taken with the apartment, though baffled by a particular brand of Swiss austerity that seemed at odds with Gudrun's elegance and Teddy's flamboyance. On my first visit there, I was struck by the fact that the other guests were all single. A woman named Jane stood out particularly, sporting a red bow tie and wearing a suit. She worked in a bookstore along Charing Cross Road and clearly knew her way around the house better than the other dinner guests. Once again, as in Beijing, Teddy was off giggling with some chaps in a corner.

As my friendship with the couple grew, all was revealed. The pillar of Amex and Ingrid Bergman were both gay, the former ensconced with a Spaniard younger than his son, and the latter partnered with the bibliophile in the bow tie. In their fashion, Teddy and Gudrun were devoted to each other, having carved out separate lives that permitted them to continue sharing one.

An invitation from Gudrun was irresistible—even if it was to a distilled concert version of Birtwistle's *Gawain*. Julian and I met up with Gudrun and Jane at the Albert Hall and found our way to a box, where Gudrun graciously laid on food and drink. Much to my surprise, the pleasure continued after the lights went down. The concert version, streamlined by canny editing, drew me in, with extraordinary sounds made by the orchestra arrayed right beneath our box. And then came the interval.

I made a dash for the loo, less out of desperation than a desire to avoid a scrum. Despite my haste, there was already a full house before the massive porcelain Victorian urinals. Finally in place before one, I became aware of a boffin to my left, covered in gray polyester of different shades. There was his odd coif, too, which began to move, sliding off his head and into the drain-pan below.

I tore out of that toilet like the wind, managing to zip up but barely able to stifle hysterics until just outside the door. Back at my seat, I told the others what had happened, much to their delight. For the rest of the concert I lamely stifled naughty giggles, which proved contagious to the ladies and Julian. Even in the dark I tried combing the audience, looking for a man with no toupee or a wet one, who was struggling even harder than I was to pay attention to the music.

THE DEATH OF DIGNITY

Turning forty had been tough. My father had died shortly before my birthday, and the frustration of unfinished business had informed the occasion. By contrast, turning fifty was a walk in the park. It was at this milestone that Confucius had observed, "Man understands the biddings of the cosmos." Though not yet evolved to such heightened sensitivity, I was now Hattie's father, a role that leaves just about everything else in the dust. Life, though, got even better with the coming of baby Tillie. Julian and I had traveled a long way, indeed, since meeting up at that Chelsea pub years before. Our adventuresome partnership now included parenthood.

As a matter of course, I had my yearly checkup at this time. No problems were discovered, although my doctor told me a colonoscopy was advisable. He highly recommended a Harley Street consultant, so I made an appointment. In advance of it, a large envelope arrived with instructions and various packets of powders to be taken at specific intervals prior to the procedure. I was also asked to decide upon the level of sedation I preferred. If I chose to be completely knocked out, someone would have to pick me up. Since Julian, an opera composer, was going to be out of London for a performance of one of his pieces, I concluded that a muscle relaxant would be just fine. I was actually a bit curious about the procedure, though disgusted by it as well.

After arriving at the clinic weakened by the prescribed ablutions, I was whisked into a cubicle, where I slipped into a hospital gown and awaited my turn. The curtain to my left was suddenly swept back, making way for a gentleman on a gurney who had obviously just been through the procedure. As he was awake, I gathered he had chosen the muscle relaxant option, too. Once settled down he mumbled a bit, leaving me unsure about whether conversation was being initiated. I made some comforting noises back, which seemed to please him. Rising up on my elbow and facing him, I took a good look as he lay there, discovering it was the chap without the teddy bear from *Brideshead Revisited*! There was something leveling about our nether innards being explored by the same physician, I thought. And then I was wheeled away.

The doctor, an older gentleman, was a stand-up comedian. With my muscles now relaxed, I was able to watch the monitor, wondering about the camera now navigating within me. At one point, he asked me to stop giggling at his jokes, as my good humor was holding up the procedure.

As he finished, pronouncing me healthy, he offered to share a confidential bit of information: "Do you realize that your large intestine is about thirty percent larger than that famous fellow's out there?"

After being returned to my cubicle, I was a bit disoriented.

My neighbor, who was preparing himself for departure, kindly asked how I was feeling.

Thanking him for his inquiry, I then told him that I had some disturbing news to relay. Turning the doctor's secret on its head, I said, "Do you realize that your large intestine is thirty percent smaller than mine?"

He roared with laughter and left, his career unharmed by the handicap.

WARWICK

During my first trip to Sydney, I attended a playboy's wedding. Paul—the dim, strapping, transplanted womanizer—was marrying a glamorous, horsey heiress from Waga Waga. I was invited not only as a guest but as Paul's stand-in at the office, since the couple would be away for a long honeymoon.

As I found my stride in Sydney, exploration of local watering holes was *de rigeur*. During one evening's pub crawl, I met a fellow named John, whose suspenders were as colorful as his spectacles. Angular and tall, he worked in the entertainment business, concentrating on children, a focus that naturally commanded my attention. Our friendship survived my departure from Australia, and we managed to see each other in various venues around the world, in addition to speaking from time to time on the phone.

One day John called me in my London flat, where music was blasting through the wide-open windows onto Oakley Street. He had a favor to ask. His cousin Warwick, a physician, was retiring. Diagnosed with AIDS, he would be taking one last trip around the world and needed an address in London to which medication and syringes could be sent. I agreed, insisting only that the contents of the package be truthfully declared to avoid any discovery of misrepresented goods.

The box arrived, and Warwick soon called, keen to pick

it up. I invited him to brunch, expecting a version of John. Rather, he was a pasty little man with whom conversation was uneasy. Warwick, a permanent expat from Australia, had worked for the World Health Organization around the globe. As an older gay man living simultaneously out of the closet and anonymously in the world, his shadowy and itinerant lifestyle suited him.

Though disappointed by the encounter, I expected to be occasionally in touch with him during his London sojourn, but with the package gone things went quiet. Julian and I caught sight of him once at the Festival Hall, very much on his own but apparently enjoying the evening; we saw no reason to intrude. According to John, he was about to make a side trip to Turkey.

On a bright, sunny Saturday several weeks later, the phone rang. A barely audible voice said simply, "I need you to bring me lemonade."

It was Warwick. He was staying at the Sheraton in Knightsbridge. I just knew that by agreeing to his request my involvement in a drama was assured. I set off to pick up the lemonade—called Sprite in the United Kingdom—and then went to the hotel.

When I inquired at the hotel's front desk, I was immediately surrounded by members of the staff expressing concern about the gentleman on the executive floor. He had not been out of his room for a week, nor had he let anyone in for three days. Though a virtual stranger, I was now cast as Warwick's representative. A manager escorted me up to Warwick's floor, its luxurious interior eclipsed by my anxiety over what I might find. In the early years of the AIDs epoch, the unknown was even more frightening than the reality.

I knocked on the door, and a voice told me to go away. I announced my name, which did not seem to register. I then uttered the word *lemonade*. Secretly hoping that I could escape the scene, my heart sank as the door opened ever so slightly.

"Come in by yourself," Warwick whispered.

It took some time for my eyes to adjust to the darkness, the curtains having been drawn tight. The large bed was in disarray, and food carts stacked with plates were parked about the room. Warwick hunched before me, barely distinct from the chaos surrounding us. I gently steered him toward a chair, half expecting my arm to pass right through his emaciated torso, unsure that somebody was even there. We sat, knee to knee, my sole aim being his evacuation to Westminster Hospital, where he was known to the doctors. Despite his sad shape, he was resolute in not wanting to leave the hotel. Though I was sympathetic to his stubbornness, understanding his fear that only the hotel might be standing between him and death, I could see he needed urgent medical attention. It took hours to talk him into going to the hospital.

The hotel staff was ecstatic, assuring me that Warwick's things would be safely stored. It was dusk as we emerged from the Sheraton. After settling him into the hospital, I was finally able to leave, drained by such intimate contact with a stranger.

Julian and I, very much a team, made alternating visits to Warwick's hospital room, though neither of us felt welcomed by him. We often sat in silence with the patient, who occasionally made a request, releasing us from awkward captivity. The staff treated us like Warwick's family, and we gradually got to know the families of other patients, all of us dreading the endgame of our vigils. I was in regular contact with John back in Australia, all the more often as Warwick's decline accelerated.

During our breaks in the waiting room, the staff offered us tea or coffee, and a biscuit. The pleasure of nibbling on that biscuit, balanced on the saucer, went far beyond the biscuit itself. It came to represent a refuge from my vigil for a stranger who was going to die. Then one day the biscuit was missing. Thinking it had simply been forgotten, I asked Maureen, the feisty Irish nurse, for one of the chocolate ones.

"No more biscuits, darlin'," she chirped. "The NHS has put a stop to them."

The grind of Warwick's decline was made all the more difficult by his emotional detachment. I was with him when he died. After the doctor covered his body, I took comfort in the notion that I had not let Warwick die alone. What finally enabled me to leave him was the realization that I actually knew nothing about him, and that he might not have needed me at all. Was I, in fact, the needy one? I wondered.

As I emerged from the room, Maureen appeared at my side suggesting that we chat in her office. Citing the kind attention that Julian and I had shown to Warwick, she revealed insight into our curious relationship with him.

"Now that he has passed, it is time for you to step away. Otherwise, your lives will be taken over by paper. It's one thing to pay heed to a person—even if you don't know him well. But why get involved with lawyers?"

She handed me a piece of paper naming several of the hospital administrators for the family to contact. She then offered me a slice of soda bread still partially wrapped in foil. We chatted quietly about life beyond the hospital. As she sent me on my way, I thanked her and asked what I could do for the hospital.

"Bring us our biscuits back," she replied half-jokingly.

By the time I arrived home, it was getting dark. I turned on all the lights, uneasy about being alone. Remembering that Jews customarily wash their hands after attending a funeral, I did the same, hoping the ritual might relieve my anxiety. Now I had to notify John of his cousin's death. It turned out that he had gone on holiday somewhere in Queensland. Hours later, after I had been playing long-distance sleuth, John called me. Clearly in holiday mode, he matter-of-factly listened to the news, saying little back to me. When I suggested that it was time for the family to take over, he said that he was on vacation and still needed my help with hospital authorities, sounding put out by my stepping aside. I apologized at first, getting pencil and paper ready to take down his next instructions. Then Maureen's words came to mind. I put down the pencil, telling John that I could no longer be involved and asking him to take down the number of the hospital contact to sort out the situation. Grudgingly, he did so and hung up.

Thereafter, once a month on a Saturday morning I would ride my bike to Waitrose, fill up the panniers with biscuits, and deliver them to Maureen. My routine continued well after the hospital had moved to new premises and Maureen was long gone. I would then give the bags of biscuits to anyone sitting at the desk in the AIDS ward, brushing aside their interest in me. I did not stop the ritual until we moved to Hong Kong a few years later.

VENDETTA

A French photographer on a global tour to chronicle the Jewish diaspora was coming to Hong Kong, my new bank posting. I received a letter from the Reform synagogue inviting me to a meeting where details would be provided. On the appointed evening, I left The Peak for the United Jewish Congregation, which was hidden away within one of the many mid-level apartment towers hovering above the harbor. I entered a stark room that was more in keeping with a Danish motel than a synagogue.

A congregant described the photographer's grand plans. There would be *tableaux vivants* in traditional Chinese costumes, shoots at various scenic spots, and a photograph of the local Jewish community, Reform and Orthodox, arrayed along the facade of the Orthodox Ohel Leah Synagogue. It had been constructed in 1901 by the Sassoons, a legendary Sephardic family, and named to honor the clan's matriarch. This finely plastered building, with its colonial and baroque features, radiated candlelight through its stained-glass windows. Although the congregation was Sephardic, with music unknown to me and lots of food with spinach and cheese, the romance of the place held out great appeal. But I checked too many boxes to be eligible for membership. There was no way that a gay father of an adopted Chinese daughter with another on the way could pass muster; nonetheless, since it *felt* like a synagogue I still had warm feelings for the place and was happy to live a benign life alongside it.

Barely had the speaker fallen silent when those in the front started peppering her with questions about the first two scenarios described. It was only after their frenzied inquiry that the photograph of the community was discussed. The picture would be in black and white, but all participants were required to wear identical red Mao jackets that could be ordered by special arrangement from a local tailor who was invariably styled as Shanghainese; for reasons neither explained nor understood, monochrome photography was best served by this brightest of colors.

I was keen to be part of the event and noted the date for jacket measurement—one for me and one for Hattie, who had just broken her leg after jumping off the top of bunk beds. My tiny girl was now burdened with a cast. I had kept her with me the night of the mishap, and she had inadvertently hit me in the head with her plastered leg.

A few days later, a woman with a heavy French accent called and identified herself as the photographer's assistant. Having heard about our two-father family, she expressed his interest in meeting us, in the hope of arranging a session to capture us as a special part of the project. I immediately invited them to supper.

On the appointed evening, the doorbell rang, and she entered first, more like a secret service agent than a guest.

Once in the flat, she jerked her severely coiffed and hennaed head around, signaling to the photographer. He then sauntered in, gliding about at his leisure, oddly managing to avoid our view of the harbor.

After we were all around the table, the evening turned jolly. We heard many tales of far-flung Jewish communities and interesting details of the photographer's recent trip to Samarkand, a place Julian and I had visited when Uzbekistan had barely been cut loose from the crumbled Soviet Union. Several plans were also hatched for us to be photographed around Hong Kong. Our guests' interest in us was only heightened when we showed them a picture of our second daughter, who had yet to leave China.

During our sojourn in Hong Kong, adoption from the Mainland was possible. I had gotten it into my head that being an only child was not a good thing, having been one myself; thus, we had applied for another child not long after Hattie's arrival. That Julian had been an only child as well, saw nothing wrong with it, and was still recovering from the shock of parenthood—though an instant hit as a father— escaped my notice.

As the evening drew to a close, our guests turned theatrical again, with the assistant, on the hoof, snapping random photographs of us. It reminded me of an evening long ago in Hong Kong, when I had been one of Andy Warhol's minders on Halloween.

Over the course of the next few days, I inadvertently

learned of a smear campaign that had been waged against my family by the Orthodox rabbi of Ohel Leah. The flash point had been the Reform rabbi's naming of Hattie in the synagogue at the time of her adoption. It was of great import to me that our girl be woven into the cloth of life; a welcoming ceremony into a tradition of G-d seemed only natural. Clearly, though, my own respect for the rules of orthodoxy and the warmth I had felt for a charming building were not enough to keep me out of harm's way.

I lamely tried to dismiss such fundamentalism as someone else's right, delving deep into my own reserve of goodwill to tolerate hatred. It didn't work. My child was being endangered by a man using G-d as a cudgel against me and mine.

The Orthodox rabbi's besmirching of the Reform rabbi's joyous sanctification of my girl plagued me and had to be addressed, but now was not the time for impassioned prose committed to paper. Written words would be dismissed by the zealot, and I did not have the stomach to confront him, fearing that I might either sob or resort to violence.

I opted for spite. One evening I climbed the steep path to the summit of The Peak and went to the Park 'n' Shop. In the biscuit department, I searched for a big box containing lots of individually wrapped packets. Then I started reading the ingredients. My choice finally made, I returned home.

On the appointed day of the photograph, the taxi arrived, and I juggled Hattie and her cast in my arms, along with the ever-present baby bag, the biscuits, red jackets, and framed photo of Tillie, our second daughter, still in Luoyang. Once at the old synagogue (called "Jew Club" by the taxi driver when given the address in my hopeless Cantonese), we quickly located Nigel, an English barrister, and his daughter Hannah, and Ali, an English entrepreneur, and her daughter Grace. They were dear friends who would gather at our flat each Sunday, where the girls were a giggling troika of competing fairies bouncing on beds.

We busied ourselves getting the children into their jackets, a task made all the more difficult by Hannah and Grace's fascination with Hattie's cast. Finally kitted out, the little girls huddled around Hattie, who was seated on a folding chair. I then asked Nigel and Ali if they would look after my girl for a few minutes. Naturally, they assumed I was off for a slash. I grabbed a paper bag and left. Once in the deserted synagogue that I had entered from our outside perch above the main level, I sat in a pew and began fumbling with the biscuit box. Separating the individually wrapped packages, I rose and began secreting them beneath the benches and in shelves holding prayer books along the pews. Having swiftly gone about my appointed rounds, I left to rejoin the group.

The photographer was theatrically barking instructions through a Tannoy, ensuring artful placement of participants along the facade on all levels of the building. Our group already occupied a fine niche on one of the terraces. With Hattie in my arms, I then reached into the bag for Tillie's photograph and held it aloft in my free arm.

The photo opportunity was quickly over, and we all agreed to meet at our flat on Barker Road. Back in a taxi in our red jackets, I took pleasure in my subversive act of defiance, but lingering respect must have prevented my opening the individual plastic packages of biscuits containing lard. I left no crumbs. Nonetheless, the gesture was enough. The liberal New Yorker within me then suddenly reared up. I had placed the *traif* tokens only upstairs, where women, other victims of orthodoxy, were penned in by their menfolk.

THE DOMINATRIX AND
THE ELVES

Stuck in the corner of yet another dreary Hong Kong reception, I found myself near a bland-looking gentleman. Out of courtesy, I acknowledged him, and he matched my glance with kindred sloth. Somehow our shared lack of enthusiasm broke the ice, prompting us to confess that duress had accounted for our presence at the event.

We exchanged cards like courtly mannequins. But children, rather than the usual Hong Kong small talk—real estate, holiday destinations, the stock market, and the British handover of the colony's sovereignty—soon took over our conversation. Richard was, in fact, the adoptive father of four from Hong Kong and Thailand, and I was blessed with Hattie and baby Tillie, who had just arrived from Luoyang. We swiftly became action figures, chatting about children whose photos seemed to fly from hand to hand. That's how our friendship began.

The youngest of Julia and Richard's children was Talia, whose eyes reminded me of a Keane painting. That she and Hattie were the same age accelerated the relationship developing between our two families. Playdates grew regular, with the girls gravitating to the flowers and pets on Talia's roof garden.

One autumn evening, as the girls were playing and the

adults were sipping gin and tonics, Julia mentioned that she was planning an event for an organization of professional women that she chaired. Since it would be held at Christmastime, she suggested that Talia and Hattie distribute party favors to the guests. I expressed enthusiasm, reckoning that exposure to accomplished women could only be good for three-year-old Hattie, the daughter of two fathers.

On the appointed day, I picked Hattie up at her Montessori school on Caine Road, and we went to a private room at the American Club in Exchange Square. Julia greeted us with her endearing warmth and pep, making a big fuss over Hattie's party frock, about which the toddler was, at best, indifferent. Julia explained that Talia would be briefly delayed as Richard had been late in picking her up at school. Hattie and I shared disappointment—she missed her pal, and I wasn't keen on being the only "boy" in the house. Julia then led us graciously to her table in the very front of the long dining room, immediately before a raised platform.

I looked around the room with Hattie sitting on my lap. It was impossible not to notice the preponderance of elegant Indians swathed in saris and crisp Chinese dressed in fitted black suits and dripping in lunchtime diamonds; Western women, despite their significant number, were somehow reduced to mere foils for the colors and bling of the locals. Some of the self-aware ladies surprisingly allowed themselves to cluck over my daughter, displaying incongruous warmth. As I was basking in Hattie's celebrity status, Julia was suddenly at the lectern welcoming her guests, with the two chairs beside us, meant for Talia and Richard, still empty. She then briefly went on to introduce an entertainer and returned to our table.

The headliner strode out, dressed in a black peignoir covering a red corset and black fishnet stockings and wearing a Santa Claus hat. She had a sack hoisted over her shoulder that she casually dropped to the floor, its sex toys tumbling out. On her way to this gig, she must have cleaned out the fetish shop under the Escalator for her party favors. I felt like we were at opening night of *Springtime for Hitler*, so stunned was I by this alien routine. I immediately lifted Hattie and made for the door amongst the seated women who, shocked, seemed to have lost the power to blink.

We were soon standing in the lobby, Hattie confused and I relieved. Suddenly the elevator opened, whereupon Talia and Richard bounded toward us, filled with regret about their delay. The girls immediately held hands and ran toward the door to join the festivities. As Richard looked on in amazement, I nearly dove before them to thwart their progress. All he could focus on was their tardiness, which he feared might deny Talia her role as Hattie's fellow Christmas elf.

I quickly explained the situation to Richard, allowing the girls to continue frolicking in the anteroom as we waited for the performance to end. It was not applause that provided the "all clear" sign. Rather, Julia rushed out to usher us back in. It was time for Hattie and Talia to hand out the presents. They were soon on the very stage that moments before had been occupied by that woman and her vibrating devices, but now Julia was nervously sending the little girls amongst the women who had regained control of their eyelids.

THE TRAGEDY QUEUE

I had heard the story so many times: my uncles and cousins were at Yankee Stadium on a Sunday when an announcement was made over the public address system summoning all men in uniform to report for duty at the nearest armory. Despite growing bored with this oft-repeated tale, I took notice that the passage of years in no way diminished either the detail or intensity in its telling. The bombing of Pearl Harbor on December 7, 1941, described by President Roosevelt as "a day that will live in infamy," happened well before I was born; nonetheless, it continued to loom large until a bright autumn Friday in 1963.

I was on my way to English class at Bronx Science. Mrs. Berson was out, so we would get a respite from *The Autobiography of Lincoln Steffens.* As I walked toward her classroom, I noticed Mr. Katz holding a transistor radio close to his ear. Paying this sports nut little mind, I assumed he was tuned into some athletic event, which meant nothing to me. In the classroom, my desk partner Neil was already seated, keen to tell me about his weekend plans. In response to his news of being Broadway-bound to see a musical, I complained that duty would take me to a bar mitzvah of some unknown cousin in the wilds of Brooklyn. Students continued to wander in, with the room growing surprisingly silent the more crowded it became, the hushed tone all the stranger in the absence of a teacher.

Then the substitute came in, stood in silence before Mrs. Berson's desk, and announced, "Something has happened to President Kennedy in Texas, and we are waiting for details."

A hand sprung up in the back. It was Ladle Lips, our nickname for Steven, a humorless bridge player who was asking about some tax policy. His surreal query elicited a collective groan of resignation amongst our classmates. Before Ladle Lips could be seated, we noticed a man nearing the flagpole in the courtyard at the school's entrance. Once there, he untied the knotted rope at the bottom and began lowering the flag. As this was happening, the public address system crackled to life, with Dr. Taffel, our principal, announcing that President Kennedy had been assassinated in Dallas and that we were to return home immediately. In the hall, rumors were rife: Vice President Lyndon Johnson had suffered a heart attack; he was dead; Mrs. Kennedy had been shot; there was a plot against the government . . .

Out on the street and walking in groups, we were silent, even making it across Villa Avenue without being taunted by the Italian toughs who regularly called us "Science fags." No one stopped at the candy store on the Concourse en route to the subway. Shortly after I arrived home, my mother appeared, having left work early. She announced that we would not be going to Aunt Marcy's house for supper, thereby departing from an inviolable Friday night tradition.

I had been a volunteer for Kennedy, his candidacy coinciding with my first real awareness of politics. When he had passed our house on the Concourse in a motorcade, I managed to snap a photo of his fleeting limousine with my Brownie. The urgency of his candidacy had been heightened by his contrast to Richard Nixon, a man intensely disliked by members of my family. It was one thing to prefer Stevenson to Ike and quite another to disapprove of Mr. Nixon. My relatives made puzzling comments about a dog called Checkers, a lady named Helen Gahagan Douglas, Nixon's wife's cloth coat, and Senator Joseph McCarthy, none of which yet explained to me the visceral reaction he inevitably aroused. My mother also gave no credence to comments about JFK's Catholicism, which some bigots suggested might indirectly place the pope in charge of our government.

There were many phone calls the next day about whether the unknown cousin's bar mitzvah reception would still be held and if we would go. Ultimately my mother, aunt, uncle, cousin, and I all drove to Brooklyn, with none of the bickering that usually attended a drive to that alien borough. The silence continued as we entered the catering establishment where relatives and friends had gathered, everyone uneasy about the event with tragedy looming so large.

A rabbi helped steer us to a place that allowed for celebration alongside the death of our president. After all, there was holiness in ritual itself. The rite of passage for which we had gathered was not to be diminished by death, nor would death be trivialized by the celebration. He called for a moment of silence, and then, gradually, the room quickened, with guests often looking to the rabbi as though needing cues from someone empowered to loosen the reins of grief. He was not only generous on behalf of the bar mitzvah boy, but understood that the guests needed his help as well.

We got home long after midnight, our exhaustion a relief from the drama of the president's death, but that did not prevent my getting up early, as usual. I filled a bowl with Raisin Bran, to which I added both milk and a bit of coffee, and went into the living room to watch television. A suspected assassin had been tracked down the day before in Dallas and was now being transferred from one secure facility to another. In these Cold War days, that he had once lived in Russia—the only thing supposedly known about Lee Harvey Oswald thus far—certainly focused attention on him. As he was being led away, a scuffle broke out almost immediately, denying me any time to have a good look at this man who might have done such a horrifying thing. Then he was shot dead right on TV by a night club owner named Jack Ruby, who had found his way into this restricted area. I made little sense as I awakened my mother, whose sleep that morning had to have been all the more valued, her usual working week fatigue compounded by the late-night return from Brooklyn and the sadness of events.

The tail of this tragedy was a long one, with the subsequent assassinations of Martin Luther King and Robert Kennedy both bound up in it. November 22, 1963, radiated out from the calendar like December 7 had for so long; it remained that way until I went school hunting in London decades later.

Julian, our daughters, and I were by then living in Japan, but it was no place for a freelance opera composer to thrive. The local music establishment could not make sense of an individual out of the box. So when I was offered a new position in London, I grabbed it. For me, the time in Tokyo had been a bit short. I was on the cusp, yet again, of linguistic comfort, but the quality of my Japanese was not what life was all about.

I traveled to London to find us a place to live and check out the schools. On a bright September day, I had breakfast with a new colleague inherited in the Chase purchase of J. P. Morgan. A slight Frenchman with airs and graces, he chose to enlist the excessive splendor of the Ritz to enhance his own value, putting me on notice that he might consider reporting to me—but only on paper. I let my height and the gravitas of my double-breasted pinstriped suit speak for me. The ordeal over, I was then met outside by an educational consultant who had arranged for me to call on some schools. After seeing two, neither of which impressed me, I took a taxi back to my hotel near Piccadilly Circus. Approaching my destination, the cabbie mumbled something about a mishap in New York, his words so vague that I paid them little attention. By the time I entered the lobby, I knew something was wrong. There had been an accident at the World Trade Center, people were saying—it had just been hit by a plane. I dashed upstairs and turned on the television. And there, right on the screen, one of the towers was clearly gashed by a plane. Despite the time difference, I immediately called Julian in Tokyo, telling him to turn on the TV, and we both watched as the second plane hit the other tower.

Julian and I spoke several more times that day, with few words actually passing between us. After our last conversation, I felt uneasy in my room, with the constant replay of the collapsing towers both hypnotic and sickening. So I went off to the gym, its only available Stairmaster right next to a particularly rude colleague of mine named Jorge who happened to be in town. To my surprise, he interrupted his workout and began a conversation, keen to tell me where he had been earlier that day when tragedy had struck. He, too, apparently did not want to be alone, and went on to reveal a warmth and compassion that allowed me to suffer his subsequent lapses. When I suddenly remembered that I had a supper appointment with my friend Nick, I left abruptly, asking that he forgive my hasty departure and telling him that I was pleased we could be together at such a time.

There was silence at Kensington Place, lacking its usual edge. Though Nick and I were glad to see each other, and he expressed pleasure at the news that I would be returning to London, we seemed, like all the others there that evening, trapped in our table reservations. We parted early, and he saw me off in a taxi.

As I alighted from it in front of the hotel and was paying the driver, he took my hand when returning the change, expressing sympathy and saying, "Tonight we are all Yanks. G-d bless."

I saw a few more schools the next day, breaking down in tears when told at one appointment that at the Changing of the Guard at Buckingham Palace the band had played "The Star-Spangled Banner." One particularly fine school, which happened to be a stone's throw from the Libyan Embassy, got short shrift. To be sure, the stress of our new world could hardly be avoided in such a place.

The British Airways flight back to Tokyo was almost empty, and the staff, sensing my discomfort, was as surprisingly warm as Jorge had been in the gym. It was as though they were on suicide watch, with people taking turns sitting beside me. I might have been doing them some good as well, as several expressed dread at being en route to Japan at a time like this.

My recollections of JFK's assassination will never be imprinted on Hattie and Tillie. Pearl Harbor has been demoted even further, now at the back of a lengthening queue of tragedies remembered personally by fewer and fewer people, receding in memory through the velocity of time. While I struggle to avoid images of the Twin Towers, I dread the inevitable demotion of 9/11 upon its eventual replacement by a tragic successor.

SEDER IN KENSINGTON

A new position at the bank prompted my sudden invitation to a management meeting. I knew most of my new colleagues, but Mike was a stranger whose reputation—as an Irish-Catholic ex-Marine from Brooklyn who had taken no prisoners—put me off.

A charismatic facilitator took charge at our very first session, having been brought in by D'Arcy, the big boss, to address dysfunction in the ranks. The opening exercise required each of us to discuss feelings about one of the other participants. While I cannot recall what I said, my routine blended circumlocution with passive-aggression and was quizzically received, but Mike's comment startled me.

"I'm afraid of Peter," he confided.

During these early days, we had little contact. I was based in Hong Kong, happily back in the Far East. Mike was up to his epaulets in the details of running a mammoth business on West 33rd Street, across the road from a diner that served buffalo burgers. Our paths did occasionally cross, but the fear to which he had confessed was never in evidence. In fact, after seeing him in action with others I judged his thuggish reputation to be accurate.

One of my routine trips to New York for a professional tune-up coincided with D'Arcy's departure from the bank.

The management team to which I belonged was summarily summoned. In a funereal conference room, Don, the cerebral and brusque vice chairman, announced that Mike was being named temporary head of the entire business—but had less than a 10 percent chance of being given the job permanently. He went on to say that headhunters were already snapping at his ankles to land the search assignment. Don's performance abruptly over, he left us staring at each other around the big wooden table.

Mike's first words filling the vacuum, navigating between the triumph of getting the job and the humiliation of likely not keeping it, showed me the mettle of the man. Clearly, that 10 percent waved before him like a red rag to a bull, but, unlike a bull, he understood that diplomacy coupled with results might just tip the scales in his favor down the road. He then graciously saw me off to Hong Kong.

His rigor was soon felt on the other side of the earth. Notoriously intimidated by numbers, I came to fear him less than I feared having my shortcomings exposed. I was determined, though, to learn how to deliver the goods to Mike's satisfaction. Then a sudden opportunity was offered to me in Japan that meant a disruptive move for Julian and the girls. I was sure, though, that they would love the places of my edited student memories: Asakusa's Edo-like charm, the Moss Garden in Kyoto, and the lights of Ginza. Extrication from Hong Kong was not easy, however, with Julian now the voice of classical music at RTHK, the local radio station, and the children happily at school. Furthermore, I was uneasy about discussing my personal life with Mike. But my big moment on the phone to discuss issues concerning Julian, Hattie, and Tillie was greeted by Mike's sweet expression of eagerness to meet my family and a pledge to ensure an easy transition. I was also to let Julian know that the loss of the radio gig was truly taken on board and profoundly appreciated.

If only Sacred Heart, the school in Tokyo so highly recommended, had been as welcoming. Based on the positive experiences of valued friends in Tokyo with the school, I wrote off for applications, which swiftly arrived in Hong Kong. Since a family photo was required, I decided to make an appointment to see the head of the lower school on my next visit to Japan. That she turned out to be a butch Australian redhead put me at ease about the school's broad shoulders, but ultimately she did not inform the process. I was finally told by Sister Ogawa, the aged headmistress, that our applications could not be considered. That a woman of G-d could victimize my babies saddened me deeply. Mike heard about what had happened and expressed not only anger but shame. Since then I no longer visit St. Patrick's Cathedral and light candles, as I had done my whole life as a New Yorker rather than a Catholic.

We made it to Japan, with the girls happily settling into the Tokyo International School, its principal proudly wearing us like a badge. But my professional landscape was swiftly altered with the announcement of yet another merger. Very soon waist-deep in its blood and charged with the sale of a problematic bank license, I was now in touch with Mike frequently, dealing with issues that challenged my bandwidth, but we got through it. As it happened, the successful sale of the license coincided with Mike's permanent promotion to the big job and his need for a trusted sidekick in London. Though unexpected, for me it was like going home since I had lived there for over a decade, and Julian did a jig to be leaving Japan.

Returning to London as a father as well as an alien amidst the J. P. Morgan grandees who had managed to commit professional suicide without tarnishing their firm's name, I realized that the world was new despite the landmarks of a past life. At least at the outset, my height, linguistic exoticism, and Ede and Ravenscroft suits eased my way amongst the bankers, but sorting out the girls' religious education was not so easy. Relying on my friend Philip, who, in a moment of weakness, had told me that his Hebrew name was Fivish, I compiled a list of synagogues with Sunday schools, some of which were held on Saturdays. My first appointment was in west London. Since the categories of Orthodox, Conservative, and Reform lacked significance in England, I was guided by description rather than label as I went about my inquiry.

The ebullient rabbi, an American who had been in London for decades, was more than welcoming. Though admiring his disregard for the puzzling niceties of English life, I was also ill at ease, quickly realizing that his presentation would have caused me discomfort just about anywhere. Nonetheless, I launched into my speech about our being a special family with two fathers and how taking the girls into the school would be taking us all into the community. For a moment, I was delighted by the way he summarily dismissed my anxiety with a wave of his beefy arm, but then he mysteriously launched into a very detailed description of his recent hip replacement surgery, ending with, "My doctor, who attends the orthopedic needs of the Queen Mother, is a transsexual."

He then sat back, like the Cheshire Cat, expecting recognition of his street cred. We ended up at another synagogue, opposite Lords in St. John's Wood.

Because Mike was highly organized, he notified my assistant Sue of a visit he was planning well in advance of the April date. She mentioned it in passing, and I paid little attention to the news. I asked only that she invite him to my home for supper on an evening when he was not busy with clients. Then, as the day drew near, I noticed that the date he had chosen coincided with Passover. Why not simply invite Mike to join us at our Seder, chronicling the Exodus? Parker, my closest friend at the bank, and Camille, his splendid Indo-American wife, were already coming.

Early on in my second London tour it was my good fortune to learn of a talented woman who was interested in jumping ship and coming to work at J. P. Morgan. Since Betty was well known in the market, our first meeting was a clandestine affair at a hotel near St. Catherine's Dock. I told her that recognizing me would be simple: a chap on crutches sporting a leg brace, on the mend from recent knee surgery. She offered no clues.

Into the lobby I hobbled, barely able to focus on my reason for being there, but it did not take long to be warmed by the beatific glow coming from the baby-faced woman standing before me, dressed in a skirted charcoal-gray suit subverted by pink pinstripes. Our chemistry was immediate, with her expertise obvious, personality irresistible, and edge challenging. That she was a big northern lass and appeared to be a lesbian enhanced the pleasure and complexity of the package. While confident that our feelings were mutual and that each had the measure of the other, Betty, after joining the bank, truly believed that her lifestyle was a mystery. I, for one, could make no bones about being part of a two-father family, quickly understanding that if I ever hesitated about such matters I would be signaling to my children that something was wrong. It was Hattie and Tillie, rather than a diverse world, who sorted me out.

Over time, Betty and I grew close. Then, at an off-site meeting after a few cocktails, she mentioned her partner on several occasions.

"Does your partner have a name?" I had finally asked.

This English rose turned positively scarlet. She began to get up, and I feared that the moment would be lost. Shadowing her, I fell in with her pace, and in the course of our stroll she finally spoke of Rebecca. Over time, we all got to know one another.

Soon I began to think about inviting Betty and Rebecca over for Passover with Mike. He was Betty's boss, too, and it was high time that folks like us upped our profile. After gaining my assurance that the evening was not to be a gay event, Betty finally agreed to attend with Rebecca.

As the day drew near, the details of Mike's New York entourage became known to me: Conrad, a crusty and canny Yorkshireman who had been raised in a Polish-speaking community and transplanted to America; and Bo, a half-Italian gay preppy whose deep intelligence was compromised by contorted patter. Julian and I invited Henrietta, a loquacious and posh pal from the music world who would do just fine in the mix. At the very last moment, Camille dropped out, leaving Parker solo.

I left work early on the day of the first Seder, arriving home at De Vere Gardens to be greeted by Tillie, who was waving a hammer. She was keen to smash walnuts for *charoses*, a concoction also including apples and wine that represented the mortar made by Jewish slaves in ancient Egypt. Hattie thrust her kiddie Haggadah, the text setting forth the order of Passover service recounting the Exodus, in my face, wanting to know all about the angel who would be visiting us later in the evening. But the girls receded when I looked toward the kitchen and caught sight of Julian the Agnostic wrestling with an enormous brisket that needed turning.

At dusk, our guests arrived, and we ushered them into the sitting room. A fire flickered behind a glass screen, and the metallic strands of the Indian textile covering my maternal grandmother's dining table twinkled as though woven with tiny lights. The wine glass for the angel expected by Hattie stood tall, the matzo was piled high, and the ritual plate sat in place, with editions of the Haggadah atop each setting. Around the table were seated an Irish Catholic ex-Marine, an Anglo-Pole who was married to a Jew, a lesbian couple, a straight WASP from Maine, a buxom music critic, a gay chatterbox, two Chinese girls being raised in the Jewish faith, and their fathers—one an English opera composer and the other a Jewish sinologist. When Hattie began to chant the first of "The Four Questions" part of the Seder—the central question of which is "Why is this night different from all other nights?"—I sat back and reckoned that if the visiting angel's time were parceled out according to the most creative answer to my daughter's query, he would be going no further, spending the entire evening with us.

SIMPLY MY DAUGHTER

When I met Cindy in Hong Kong long ago, she was a high-powered business executive living next door to Julian and me on Barker Road—the penultimate stop on the Peak Tram. The most time Cindy and I ever spent together was on a trip to Hanoi. We enjoyed scouring the art galleries and visiting the homes of artists as well. She was to be married to an Englishman, and she had lots of walls to fill in their new St. John's Wood home back in London.

She was now married and ensconced in that house with two daughters, and I, too, was living in London. In her neighborhood from time to time—usually on my way to or from the Liberal Jewish Synagogue where Hattie and Tillie attended Saturday school—I would admire those paintings she bought long ago.

Our daughters had grown close, and we all agreed on an excursion to Legoland, because the scale of the place seemed just right. We had heard that the rides were not overwhelming and the place would likely not be crawling with teenagers sporting tattoos and body piercings. On the appointed Sunday, their SUV pulled up early in front of our flat at 25 De Vere Gardens. Angus, Cindy's husband, was at the wheel, and we all piled in, except for Julian, who was out of town.

Our day was off to a good start, with all four girls happily giggling in the back of the car. Although Hattie later regretted her decision to ride the roller coaster—I found myself chanting to her, "Keep breathing, and just look at me"—the girls had great fun on the gentler rides. Then, after dawdling at yet another souvenir stand, I began walking across a little bridge with Hattie, Angus, and one of his girls. Not far behind was the rest of our gang. Along came Cindy and her other daughter, but without Tillie! Cindy had thought she was with me.

We ran back across the bridge to the souvenir stand where we had all last been together. I suddenly felt that everything in this miniature world was growing tall and steep around me, with my child having been swallowed up by the surrounding towers. Despite my fear, I fell silent. People gathered, asking for a description.

"Pink sweatshirt, wide-set eyes, light brown hair, her name's Tillie…," I stammered, my eyes growing moist.

A bellow came from behind me. "For Christ's sake, she's Chinese," barked Cindy.

People fanned out immediately, looking in all directions for my baby. They moved so fast, the terror of a missing child stabbing parents instantly.

As I crossed another bridge, I caught sight of Tillie in the arms of a woman. I wondered whether my baby was being rescued or abducted. Spotting me, Tillie squirmed out of the woman's grasp and ran toward me, sobbing. In tears myself, I swept her up, and we walked toward the woman who had held her. She commented about having been through the same thing herself.

Tillie was in my arms—my daughter, not my Chinese daughter. She stuck two fingers of her left hand happily in her mouth, and we went off looking for ice cream.

THE JOY OF FISHES

*B*ernard was my father's youngest brother. He was so frail at birth that his naming was postponed until his survival was assured. During this period of limbo, his grandfather died, providing him with a name, as it is the custom of the Ashkenazi Jews to name babies after the dead.

It did not take long to figure out that Bernard had severe physical problems, likely resulting from oxygen deprivation at birth. Despite irrepressible liveliness radiating from his blue eyes, he had no control over his movements, nor could he learn to speak. As his handicaps became more complex and obvious, his brothers drew even closer to him. The import of their attention grew as their mother's inability to cope with her imperfect child became more problematic. She placed too much store in looks. Even as an old woman, when my grandmother declared that someone was "homely," the pronouncement signaled dispatch beyond the pale. To the end of her days, she was never able to address Bernard's imperfection, though her love for him was profound.

When Bernard was still young, she was suddenly widowed. Pinky, her dashing husband and my grandfather, was felled by a heart attack in his thirties. A cousin recently sent me a picture of my grandparents. There Grandma stood on a dock in trousers with knife-like pleats, hugged by the towering Pinky, who was sporting a Prince of Wales plaid tweed jacket. This image of a couple right out of the movies came as a shock to me, that faded print of their day out revealing not a hint of life's dramas.

As a teenager, when Bernard could no longer be cared for at home he was moved to Goldwater Hospital on Welfare Island, now known as Roosevelt Island. It was the making of him. He insisted on a risky operation, which finally allowed him to sit in a chair, freeing him from life on his belly, where he had forever struggled to lift his head to take in the world around him. The procedure was liberating beyond its physical benefit. Now upright, his intelligence and worldliness were positively incandescent, coming to the attention of an ever-widening circle of people. He had a belated bar mitzvah and high school graduation, and went on to university in upstate New York, cared for by a dedicated attendant who specialized in looking after those with disabilities.

As a boy, I liked to visit Uncle Bernard for two reasons: first, getting to the island, and second, transport once in the hospital. In those days prior to a bridge between Queens and Welfare Island, with no cable car from Manhattan there was only one way to make the trip. My father would drive onto the 59th Street Bridge and, when halfway across, carefully pull into an awkward lane that ended in front of a great door. The door would open, and we'd drive into a dark room that was an elevator and then be lowered within the bridge's stanchion right onto the island.

As if that weren't exciting enough, once in the hospital we would find Uncle Bernard waiting for us in the lobby surrounded by his friends, telling me to "hop on, kid." In a flash, I would take my place on the footplates of his wheelchair, and we'd be pushed around the hospital gardens and halls, my uncle forever commanding, "Faster!"

Grandpa Abe, my grandmother's second husband, and Bernard became a real team, their kinship taking the pressure off Grandma. She was protected by her husband's complete assumption of the parental role, giving her distance from her son's infirmities, which enabled her to better appreciate his gifts. The more Bernard's attentions inclined toward Grandpa, the more maternal Grandma became. Although Bernard could hardly take interest either in coin collecting or wood carving, Grandpa's favorite pastimes, he benefited from Grandpa's inventiveness. Grandpa had been an engineer on the SS *Normandie* when it sank in New York Harbor. Forever tinkering with gadgets, he created a device that was attached to the bottom of a shoe, enabling Bernard to move his own wheelchair. Such independence was thrilling; they even thought about modifying the shoe to enable Bernard to type, as he had been asked to write articles for the *Village Voice*.

After Grandma was widowed again, she was swiftly ground down. Getting to Welfare Island from her home was arduous. On automatic pilot, she made the trip a few times each week, weakened by a combination of advancing age and confrontation with her son's physical disability.

Bernard's reputation as an advocate for the disabled grew beyond the hospital's walls. Very much his own man, he tenderly encouraged Grandma to cut down her trips to Welfare Island, and that respite only enhanced his luster from afar. The evolving arrangement afforded him the independence he craved and the distance she welcomed. When he occasionally raised the possibility of striking out on his own to live with nurses who had looked after him over the years, he was derailed, feeling obliged to promise his mother that he would never leave the hospital during her lifetime. I found the pact puzzling since his liberation from the hospital would have been hers as well.

When Grandma died, my father and I made the trip to the hospital to tell Bernard. It came as no surprise as he had been in constant touch with her, providing sweet stewardship during her decline. He paid particularly close attention to me, understanding my distress as she had died in my car en route to the hospital.

"When my time comes, I sure hope you don't have a tough time finding a round casket," he quipped, making fun of his contorted body.

Within a month, Bernard announced that he was leaving the hospital to live with Bernadette and her family in rural upstate New York. A black woman, she had been his nurse during his formative years and stayed close to him.

During the transition, things went quiet for while; then Bernard called. When I picked up the phone, all I first heard were his wheeze-like giggles and the sound of children in the background. When he finally managed to speak, he started telling me of the farm's beauty and the new van he had been able to buy for the family from the trust that had been put aside long ago. Throughout the conversation he was playfully shooing away kids who were tickling him. When Bernadette got on, she assured me that Bernard had settled in well, which was obvious.

Bernard had moved far away, but his presence in my life grew in significance. It had been around him that my distant father and I had been able to come together. Two such occasions stand out, but sadly did not become a continuum of experiences.

The first had occurred in the early morning following the American bicentennial. I was startled to receive a phone call from my father, as we had been out of touch for some time.

"Bernard fell out of his chair watching the tall ships on the promenade along the Hudson yesterday. His hip is broken. Meet me at Roosevelt Hospital," he commanded.

As the summons involved my uncle, I did not hesitate. Upon arriving at the hospital, I wandered around the appointed floor, finally spotting my father, who dwarfed a woman doing all the talking. As I came within earshot, the tone of their conversation at first confused me; then I realized it was Bernadette. Clearly in charge in a most intimate fashion, she was speaking as Bernard's primary relation and advocate, with my father showing her rare deference.

We were ushered into Bernard's room. There my uncle lay, suffering no spasms and looking longer as he slept. Then, as we sat around his bed, movement began beneath the blanket, and his body gradually curved. With the return of his afflictions came his power. Though delighted to see my father and me, he focused on Bernadette for assurance of his postoperative well-being. She stroked his cheek and hinted at the regimen that they would be tackling to get him over his surgery. We gingerly said our good-byes and slipped out, heartened by their relationship. I was convinced that he had done the right thing by leaving Welfare Island.

Before I had to choose between babbling and silence, my father quietly asked if I might be free for lunch. Disarmed by his gentleness, I nodded, and we walked to a neighborhood luncheonette where I often ate with my mother.

Forever a babe magnet, my father immediately attracted a waitress on whom he lavished the charm he had never gotten to use on Bernadette. We then sat in silence until our omelets came, the lady surrounding my father's plate with an array of condiments, which he playfully acknowledged. In some discomfort, I began to eat.

"Cousin Frances recently died," he announced.

I had remembered her as a kindly relative always in a bathing suit around her pool in Miami.

"Her daughters called me to drop by and pick up a valise of mine they had found in the attic. I told them just to throw it away, but they insisted that I first take a look," he continued.

Between bites I looked obliquely at my father's eyes, enlarged by his glasses and shiny with tears. I continued to eat in silence as he recounted the recovery of the suitcase.

"I was annoyed that they expected me to pick up that suitcase. Even when I got to Frances's house, I was tempted to get rid of it on the spot, but the girls insisted that it be removed. So I took the damn thing home and flung it on the bed. There was no key, so I had to force the lock open. In the bag I found correspondence with your mother, lawyers, relatives, doctors, and teachers all about you, from when you were my little Pedro. It was a sweep of your life—and it took my breath away," he acknowledged.

His alien commentary took my breath away. Lunch over, we parted, vowing to make the journey together up to see Bernard soon. That autumn, we did, resulting in the second occasion of my coming together with him. My father flew into Albany; I drove there from Middlebury, where I was teaching; and we took our road trip to rural western New York. Aside from once falling asleep on his shoulder during a long coach ride in China, I reckoned that this journey in my VW with a broken heater was the most pleasurable time I had ever spent with my father.

Bernadette's house, a decrepit and sprawling homestead, had been our destination, and it was not easy to find. As we walked toward it, we heard more and more voices, as though approaching a crowd scene. Polite knocking on the door had been a waste of time, so we finally just barged right in, and it still took a while to get noticed, despite having been seen by several people. Finally we heard Bernard, his laughter unmistakable. There he sat, in the middle of the kitchen, a bunch of giggling children climbing over him as he chatted with various adults around him. He greeted us and began irreverent and detailed introductions to everyone in the room. Bernadette soon appeared, followed by more people. This was Bernard's sprawling clan.

As food started appearing in no particular sequence, my father and I were gradually encircled by people who wanted to take a good look at us, Bernard's biological family. Peppered with questions and hugs, we were also aware of children crawling under our legs playing hide-and-seek. From time to time Bernadette's arm would enter the fray, passing one plate piled high in exchange for an empty one.

Like a balloon with a slow leak, the kitchen finally emptied, with Bernadette herding out the stragglers. Bernard seemed to await our words, making no small talk and only beaming. I immediately began raving about his new life, wondering aloud about all those years in a hospital. He brushed aside any hint of regret, saying that it had brought him valuable peace with Grandma. I then asked many questions about specific people I had just met. He was aglow as he answered, relishing my comments as acknowledgment of his new family.

My father hovered, unable to take up the slack as my exchanges with Bernard came to a natural end. Rather, he began commenting on a perilous weather report and the great distance we had to cover in traveling back to Albany. Although the two brothers had long lived very separate lives, my father identified their relationship with Bernard's life on Welfare Island. It was one thing for his kid brother to be surrounded by sick people in an institution. There was no mistaking that for home. With Bernard never really at home, my father could swoop down from time to time and reconnect with him in a shared witty patter that not only confirmed their brotherhood but demonstrated that Bernard actually belonged to him, though in a parallel universe.

It was different now, and my father knew it. This black family had happily wrapped its home around Bernard. His younger brother was no longer waiting in the front lobby of a hospital to welcome him for one of his meteoric visits. Bernard was now belonging in a way that my father could not fathom and had never accomplished in his own life. As my grandmother was dead and Bernard had a family of his own, my father, who had always kept his mother and brother at arm's length, was now cut loose. It was with my *father* as orphan that we left the farm—a unique moment in our time together.

Uncle Bernard happily drifted away from me, too. When we did speak, our chats were about his life on the farm. Bernadette would get on and assure me of his well-being. I was happy to remain quiet and hear of his pleasures. I just knew that he had gotten things right.

The brothers never saw each other again, and I'm not sure that things would have been otherwise had my father's health not deteriorated. When he died, my father's widow forgot to mention Bernard in the obituary. I did send my uncle the newspaper article from the *Miami Herald,* but I took great pains to slice off all mention of family to spare him the slight.

Just a year later, as I was about to fall asleep in London, the phone rang. It was Bernadette. Uncle Bernard had suddenly passed away, and she immediately drew me back toward the center of his life. Treating her respectfully as his next of kin, I told her to rest easy about logistics and that I would fly to New York the following day.

Much was to be done. There was one serious glitch over opening the grave at my grandmother's feet. Consent was required from an unknown but related crone in Florida who threatened to withhold her approval. I finally got to the bottom of it. She had an unfortunate history with my father and thought she was getting even by denying his brother's burial. When I assured her that my father had been well cremated a year before, she acquiesced. The funeral arrangements, with myriad choices on offer, were daunting as well. I naturally sought Bernadette's involvement, but she expressed no preferences, my gesture acknowledging her position in Bernard's life going unnoticed. Nor could I take any cues from my uncle, whose own irreverence about Judaism offered no guidance, but it was the religion that I knew. There was great relief when I finally submitted to its ritual. All seemed to flow from my insistence that my uncle's body not be left alone the night before the funeral. From that request emerged the shape of Uncle Bernard's final rite of passage. I was put in touch with a specific rabbi after mentioning that I had no interest in some happy-clappy send-off. We arranged to meet well before the service to prepare.

I arrived at the funeral parlor on Queens Boulevard early the next morning. Although my uncle did not belong to me, I wanted a bit of time alone with him. I sat in the chapel, my hand resting on the closed casket. Then a beadle came to tell me that the rabbi awaited me in a nearby room. An affable man with hair combed across his pate and covered by a skull-cap, he rose and beckoned me to sit beside him. He ceremoniously produced a tiny pencil that reminded me of miniature golf and an index card, giving the impression that he was now in command.

"Where is the family?" he asked.

I suggested that he listen to my uncle's story. As the rabbi's surprise and admiration registered, he made it clear that there would be a division of labor between us: he would see to the ritual, and I would see to the man. But nothing could have prepared him for our entry into the main chapel.

It was standing room only, filled with black people, the women dressed in an array of glorious colors and sporting amazing hats. Awaiting us in front of the coffin was Bernadette, looking both regal and mournful as she widened her arms to receive the rabbi and me. I then asked to see Uncle Bernard, and the coffin lid was lifted. His body was wrapped in simple white, and his eyes were covered with shards, more in keeping with orthodoxy than I had expected. I immediately thought back to his remark about someday needing a round coffin but was relieved to see that he was at ease, as he had been after his surgery.

It took the rabbi some time to compose himself at the rostrum, as he was both overcome and disoriented by the occasion. He did indeed see to the Jewish ritual, but then he commented haltingly on the special nature of this day, expressing regret that he had never known the man over whom he was now praying. He then introduced me.

It was not until I caught the eye of Jim, far from our days in Japan and Princeton, seated in a distant row, that I was finally able to speak. The distillation of my words appeared the following day in the *New York Times*:

> *Bernard Lighte. Devoted friend of Bernadette.*
> *Loving uncle of Peter. The elegance and success of his*
> *life is not only an example to us of what he achieved*
> *but also a potent model of what he was able to*
> *overcome. That he himself let us forget his handicap is*
> *a dim reflection of his own personal victory over it.*
> *G-d was good in putting him amongst us.*

Several months later back in London I received a letter from the monument company that my family had long used, reminding me that it was time to erect a footstone for my uncle. I was asked to confirm his details and send along any special words that I would like carved into the stone.

I know that Uncle Bernard warranted an epitaph, and I began obsessing about it. I wanted people who walked past his grave to take pause and wonder about the man who had prompted so special an inscription.

After pouring over my books and consulting various reference volumes, I came up with a list of quotations from the likes of Emily Dickinson, Will Rogers, Oscar Wilde, and Confucius—each of which missed the mark. Frustrated by my failure to get this right, I suddenly remembered Zhuangzi, the profoundly subversive and delightful Daoist who understood the inadequacy of words. "Where can I find a man who has forgotten words so I can have a word with him?" he queried.

His words would just have to do in this case. Since he had left them to us despite his own frustration with them, I knew that within his book an epitaph awaited me. I came upon his exchange with Huizi, a fellow fourth-century BC philosopher, and their parrying over the happiness of fish. Just as the Daoist master could know happiness without being a fish, so did my uncle understand life despite much of it remaining beyond his grasp.

The epitaph I faxed to the stonemason the following morning read: "I know the joy of fishes in the river through my own joy as I go walking along the same river."

ROSANNA

*B*runo, a French architect whom Julian and I each knew individually, introduced us to Rosanna. Bruno was renting a room in the rather grand flat of a decorator, and when he heard that we were looking for an occasional cleaner he recommended Rosanna, claiming that our clutter was positively Bauhaus compared to what she usually faced.

As both a large *D* and small *d* democrat, I am never comfortable having people in my employ. I always want to transform them into family members or friends regardless of their own views on equality. Straightaway I found out too much about this soft-spoken woman, her two young children, and her estranged husband, as well as their custody battles. She came only once a week but grew closer to us when Julian fell sick with hepatitis and she cooked up a storm, assuring the patient a steady diet of fresh food.

My work then took Julian and me to Hong Kong, where we adopted the girls, and on to Tokyo. After six years abroad, we returned to London with our daughters and Sonny, our dour Filipina nanny. When we all agreed it was time for Sonny to move on—there was talk of marriage to a man based in Beijing who worked for Boeing (perhaps it was the CIA)—it seemed only natural to give Rosanna a call, asking her to put out feelers on our behalf. We had stayed in touch over the years, inviting her and her children to Hattie's "coming out" party at the Polish Hearth Club on Exhibition Road, during a visit to London.

"How about me?" she immediately said when asked for recommendations.

Rosanna joined the household upon our return to London from our summer holiday on Shelter Island. Hattie took to Rosanna immediately, having long played second fiddle to Tillie on Sonny's watch, or so she thought. The kitchen was swiftly transformed into their haunt and laboratory, with Rosanna and Hattie often seen huddling over a cooking project, a piece of embroidery, or a cluster of seeds. Tillie's hovering, conducted independently, was regarded as a holding pattern rather than estrangement—after all, we were still in a period of adjustment. The smells were good, and the house hummed, giving us no reason for concern; we were relieved, in fact, that the sullen Sonny had gone her own way. But in late autumn Rosanna's unbalanced treatment of the girls became all too obvious.

Rosanna unexpectedly announced that her son Michael, a lively chap who was now a student at Imperial College, had just assembled a new bicycle for Hattie, which was to be a Christmas present. Our reactions were mixed: the extravagance of the gift could hardly be afforded by her and seemed out of keeping with the length of their relationship. She explained it away by simply saying that Hattie wanted a bicycle, but the generosity became grotesque when Rosanna mentioned, as an afterthought, that Tillie would be getting some sort of dolly. We immediately told Rosanna that we would find a second bicycle for her to give Tillie to compensate for her insensitivity to our younger daughter.

After Christmas, those bikes stood gathering dust in our entrance hall, never used by either girl and gradually becoming irritants to Julian and me as our discomfort with Rosanna grew. In fact, we eventually cooked up a plan to be rid of them. As spring approached, I suggested to the girls that their bikes on Shelter Island might now be too small for them—and that their new ones could be well-used in America. But after discovering the ridiculous cost of transport I got more creative. Offering the bikes to my pal Robert for his two sons, I insisted that they be fetched by stealth, explaining to the girls that the bikes were on their way to Shelter Island. Later, as an explanation for why they were not waiting for the girls upon our arrival, I planned to say it was due to damage en route. The ensuing drivel about the complexity of insurance, which I was obliged to offer up at the girls' insistence, so taxed my imagination that I was tempted to fess up about the whole drama. Two new bikes bought in Greenport saved the day.

Whenever doubts about Rosanna surfaced, my regard for her fine children would ease my mind. I had known Rachelle as a teenager and Michael as a little boy. At the height of Rosanna's tribulations with her husband, she kept her children close by. I would often come home in the evening, and they would be there, occupied with their homework. That Rachelle, now married to a charming Italian importer, had grown distant from her mother did not seem alarming—just the usual mother-daughter thing. When it came to Michael, Rosanna could not have been prouder—often sounding, in fact, like the mother of an only child. There was much chitchat about his upcoming university graduation and the world awaiting him. One night at supper I mentioned to him my own journey from Chinese classics to banking, suggesting the options that might present themselves to an open mind. His certainly was open, as revealed in conversations about cutting-edge solar panels in the developing world.

The flowers on our terraces were well in bloom when, one morning, I casually mentioned the timing of Michael's graduation to Rosanna. "It must be soon," I wondered aloud as I ate my grapefruit.

Rosanna responded by saying that the event had indeed already taken place the week before.

I asked for details of the occasion, to which she flatly replied, "I was not there."

Alerted to something dark, I dropped the subject and never revisited it. From then on, with our focus of the move to Beijing gaining in intensity, there was little inclination to further deepen our relationship with Rosanna. One matter remained outstanding, though. For the previous Christmas, I had done two paintings for Rachelle and Michael that incorporated the Chinese characters representing the animals associated with the years of their births. Rosanna had not been subtle about her desire for one as well. So late one Saturday night I took out my brushes and went to work on a "monkey" for her, using the colors of her native Ecuador to enliven the austere monochrome of the character. Once it had dried, I inserted the painting into a plastic sleeve and left it on her pillow, to be found upon her return from her home in Acton on Sunday night.

Like a child seeking approval, on Monday morning I climbed the steps to our rooftop kitchen to bask in Rosanna's pleasure over the calligraphy. But she didn't say a word. After going about my morning ritual, I finally asked if she liked the painting. Only the barest of acknowledgments was forthcoming. Though confused and wounded by such mystery, I took solace in the fact that it was only a matter of time before Rosanna would no longer be in our lives. I chose not to engage her, trying to remind myself yet again that, to quote Aunt Marcy, "you can't put your head on someone else's shoulders."

There was a foil for all this as well. Our landlord, Mr. Keany, had sold the flat out from under us, promising vacant possession to its new owners a few months before our actual departure for Beijing. To avoid having to move twice, I hired a lawyer to address the threat of eviction. That this whole drama seemed to have begun when Rosanna had shared our plans with the landlord fueled a growing resentment in me. This was the very same man who had not paid her for doing work in the building for him. I wondered if she, in fact, had filled him in, hoping to be paid for sharing a confidence with him. While I was unsure just how his knowledge of our plans could have affected the eviction process and of the reasons for Rosanna's indiscretion, my anxiety over the possibility of an extra move—coupled with the presence of a fifth column in our midst—was laying me low. Once the lawyer had thrown enough costly obstacles in eviction's way, I was able to once again concentrate simply on getting us out of the flat and into a temporary apartment for a week before dealing with the girls' farewells, Julian's concerts at St. Paul's Girls' School, where he was music director, and my own frenzy of extraction from J. P. Morgan at Aldermanbury.

On the last Friday night in our temporary apartment, the girls and I were watching *Doctor Who*, with Rosanna ironing nearby. We were waiting to eat the lasagna in the oven that she and Hattie had prepared for our supper while Tillie and I had been out running errands after school. We seemed suddenly to find ourselves in the scene from *The Discreet Charm of the Bourgeoisie* where the soldier suddenly presents himself, out of context, at a table of ladies, announcing, "I'd like to tell you the story of my life."

Rosanna came from behind the ironing board. Standing between my chair and the sofa upon which the girls were happily huddling, she said that she wanted to mention something and that we all needed to hear what she had to say. But her insistence did not manage to compete with *Dr. Who*; thus the girls remained oblivious to the live drama beginning to unfold.

"Tillie has been stealing my jewelry," she declared.

Though I was gobsmacked, her accusation would permit no silence. "When did this happen? What was stolen? Why would you suspect Tillie?" I shot back in a staccato whisper, reacting in this dreamlike scenario.

By now the girls were aware, indeed, of the alien performance in which we were dwelling. Tillie looked so puzzled that tears lagged behind Rosanna's attack, but Hattie sobbed immediately, somehow able to fast-forward, knowing that all was coming to grief.

When the narrative that was tumbling forth grew more and more mad—Tillie had stolen the jewelry either a year or six months before, she had spirited it off to Shelter Island, she had once been found going through Rosanna's desk—Tillie herself cottoned on not only to the fact that we were witnessing a sham but that her second-class citizenship in Rosanna's eyes was soon to be over. She thus seemed more composed than Hattie, despite the tears quietly streaming down her cheeks. With firm calmness, I tried to make sense of what was happening, but soon realized that analysis was less important than removing Rosanna from our midst. Abruptly, but quietly, calling a halt to voir dire, I told Rosanna she would have to leave immediately. She then bolted for the kitchen and removed the lasagna from the oven.

"I want my pan back," she announced, rummaging through the cupboards for a large plate on which to empty the steaming lasagna.

"Please take the whole thing. Please don't dump it out," I quietly suggested.

"No. I'll get it another time," she snapped.

Within moments she was gone, thrusting her keys at me. I immediately locked the door behind her.

I returned to Hattie and Tillie. Sitting between the girls on the sofa, I held them close, determined that they fully understand what had just transpired was about Rosanna and not them. Tillie, the accused, seemed resilient, despite the fact that the accusations had been made against her. It was Hattie who needed the attention.

"Do you think that Tillie is a thief, Xiao Qu?" I asked, using Hattie's pet Chinese name gently.

She might have expected that only sympathy at the departure of the lady with whom she had just made lasagna would have informed my words, but that would have dealt only with the edges of the drama and not its crux. It was the family that needed protection. Whatever Hattie's feelings about her little sister may have been, thievery was inconceivable; she somehow knew that tenderness coming her way over Rosanna's loss was secondary to a much larger matter with which we were all dealing.

Tillie managed to be gracious, yielding center stage to Hattie, who had had the misfortune of being taken up by a bad person.

By the time Julian got home—knackered by the rigors of rehearsing for his farewell concert—drama had seeped from the scene, leaving a quiet pall, with the girls sleepwalking through their evening rituals of snacks and teeth-brushing. It made sense to fill him in on the details only after the girls had gone to bed to avoid a needless replay, which might have wound them up. When we finally sat down alone, he was stunned by the tale. What quickly commandeered our thoughts, though, were scenarios of what might have been. Hattie and Tillie slept just fine that night, but we didn't.

For once on a Saturday morning, I was glad to be going off to religious school. Punctuality was all the more important because I was on the security rotation, requiring me to check out the synagogue's perimeter and stand at its entrance in a fluorescent jacket along with colleagues to demonstrate vigilance in our post-9/11 world.

As we were about to leave the house, the telephone rang, and Julian picked it up. It was Rosanna. I made gestures suggesting that we might delay our departure until the call was over, but Julian shooed me out of the house—much to my relief. After dropping the girls off at their class, I was told to man the front desk at reception, pushing the buzzer to admit visitors viewed on the monitor and occasionally listening to the loquacious and needy Niles, the head of security. Though not as good as sitting in Starbucks on the High Street—often passing Paul McCartney with his one-legged wife and baby along the way—I could still work on my little stories and read *The Week*. Instead, I decided to write an account of Rosanna's accusations, just in case. We would soon be leaving the United Kingdom for China, and Julian was about to adopt the girls, following our civil partnership ceremony—thus, my sudden trepidation.

As usual, the girls and I met up with Julian for lunch after synagogue. With the nonsmoking law just introduced, we found ourselves in a commodious booth at Café Med on Gloucester Road, which had long been off limits to non-smokers. In addition to the attendant hubbub of simply getting the girls settled—sorting out place mats and crayons, hearing what they did not want, and fielding inquiries about what we would be doing after the lunch we had not yet even ordered—Julian looked shaken and seemed keen for a chat. Thus as soon as the girls were finding hidden words amongst jumbled letters on their place mats, he gave me a highly edited account of the phone call, only hinting at its disturbing content. That Rosanna had identified a High Street jeweler with appropriate replacements for the stolen baubles, suggesting that they meet up that very day to right the theft, marked her ploy as blackmail. What remained unsaid heightened my anxiety in light of Julian's upcoming adoption of the girls, now only days away. Over spicy Bloody Marys, we made some decisions: to unplug the phone; alert the renter's office that Rosanna was no longer to be admitted, and do the same at J. P. Morgan; contact the lawyer handling our adoption case, a punky version of Olive Oyl and a rabid Arsenal fan named Lois; and travel as a pack on our appointed rounds. After all, Rosanna knew the girls' school bus schedule and just might show up demanding money or even with authorities, somehow interfering with the adoption and our departure. We already knew that she was not shy about involving the authorities. On one occasion, when she had determined that a dry cleaner was not honoring her laundry tickets, she had called the local council to level a complaint. When Julian then called into the shop to sort out the situation, the clerk had been beside himself, recounting tales of abuse by Rosanna, whose snide remarks about his Eastern European accent were all the more galling coming from an Ecuadorian émigré who never even produced receipts.

As we had agreed, Julian and I both arranged to be at the bus stop with the girls in the morning and afternoon. Should Rosanna appear, one of us would deal with her while the other would spirit the girls away. Then there was the sorting out of the salary legitimately owed to her. Lois sternly instructed that I was to pay Rosanna only what she was owed. After all, anything over that sum could be construed as reimbursement for stolen property, thereby acknowledging the theft. I was daunted by logistics. As I wanted to neither speak to nor see the woman again, I enlisted my trusty assistant, Sue, to arrange for the payment. But Rosanna was adamant that she would agree to nothing absent the details of the sum—which I refused to supply. Sue persevered, desisting only after Rosanna grew nasty, the details of which Sue kept from me.

My plan unfolded as I focused on the adoption proceedings to be held on the Tuesday of our last week in London. I first scrubbed the lasagna pan maniacally to a luster not seen since it was new, all the while imagining how Rosanna might have hurt the girls. I wanted no debris of her presence in our lives to exist. I then coldly took new bills and stuffed them in a dead white envelope, printed "Rosanna" on the front, and put the envelope in the pristine lasagna pan. The only carrier bag I could find was a festive green-and-foil number left over from a present to the girls, marking their departure from Hill House School. With a hint of mischief, I placed both in the party bag.

On Tuesday morning, we all got dressed up and set off in search of the door to the family court building that had been indicated in Lois's e-mail. There she was, all in black, any hint of Gothness dashed by her expansive and goofy grin. We followed her as she was bounced from pillar to post by clerks proffering conflicting directions, finally staying put in a room where we were to await a page on the public address system. In the meantime, there were still papers requiring attention. After all, our judge was said to be a notorious stickler for detail, so we might as well get everything just right.

Julian's name was called, not mine, because he was adopting my children. Since an unmarried couple of any persuasion had not been able to adopt jointly, I did it as a single parent. I saw no reason to make a political statement and end up childless. But now that civil partnership had come into its own in the UK, it was high time for Julian to become a parent of record.

When the social worker assigned to the case had previously asked one of the girls about the prospect of Julian becoming her father, she responded, with a confused look on her face, "He already is."

Although I had long regarded him as the girls' parent, my being their sole legal parent was, in fact, the last and most meaningful lever of control that remained in my possession. To tell the truth, I had taken pause as I signed documents along the way, somehow allowing myself to appear casual, all the while knowing that there were still more to be signed and a judge yet to be seen. But we were now walking into that courtroom, Julian's adoption of the girls to be finalized. I suddenly had a quick flash, imagining the proceedings as a wedding: we stood before a judge who was asking if there were any objections to the adoption—"or forever hold your peace"—and I was the one who shouted aloud, bringing a halt to it all.

Once we were really in that courtroom, though, it all seemed natural. Judge Redgrave came directly over to the girls, putting them at ease by bending down to welcome them. The first order of business was the judge's confession: what she feared would be a complex undertaking turned out to be a pleasurable experience. She sighed with relief, saying that she usually spent her time taking children away from parents rather than presiding over the creation of a happy family.

Since the underlying adoption from China had been recognized under UK law, she needed to concentrate only on Julian's petition to adopt. I was particularly glad to hear this, having taken so stern a line with social services when an investigation into my paternity of the girls was mooted. The law would have indeed been an ass, considering that Hattie and Tillie had been granted British citizenship based upon my own approved application for citizenship as their father. I was resolute that if such a probe were undertaken there would be no adoption proceedings. Instead, I had framed the situation in terms of a man whose new partner would be adopting his children. Our French social worker took this on board, and the process went forward.

It was over in minutes, and I had not even noticed that we had been reconfigured in the eyes of the law. If anything, life immediately felt lighter, but the mundane was still awaiting us. Once outside the courthouse, I took Lois aside and handed her the garish bag containing the money and the lasagna pan, asking her to deal with it. As she nonchalantly took it from me, all the while giving assurance of the ease with which matters could be handled, I sensed steeliness in her while she merrily went on her way.

Julian and the girls then took off. As his concert at St. Paul's was that very night, he would be dropping them at playdates so he could get to his rehearsal. I watched my family climb into a taxi, the usual mini-drama attending their entrance into its back prompted by Hattie's concern about who sat where. I decided to walk back to my office, feeling happily different about life. As I strolled along High Holborn, I suddenly began thinking about plants and flowers and the flat we had just left at Cornwall Gardens, its terraces heaving with greenery. I had always seemed to be watering the plants. Yet Rosanna had styled herself as the earth mother, forever saving seeds, taking cuttings, and teaching Hattie about nature. That the seeds were always in disarray on a windowsill, never to be planted, and the cuttings left to die if I did not tend to them, changed from odd to menacing as I walked along. There was hoarding of garbage as well. At times, foul smells pervaded the kitchen, the source being bags of rubbish either squirreled away in cupboards or out on the terrace. After we had once disposed of a stash, we later discovered that it had been retrieved by Rosanna from the refuse compartment at the side of the building. When we finally asked her about it, she said it was meant for her compost heap and worm farm in the garden at her Acton home.

I can only marvel at my ability to explain away flaws as quirks and mystery as scar tissue in the context of a routine that seemed to make life easy. What my complacency did, in fact, was make life dangerous for my children, those for whom my threshold for flaws and mystery should be lowest.

No doubt the worms are thriving in west London.

DUTCH TREAT

At the time of my posting to Hong Kong, Julian and I met up with a couple and their three children who seemed to adopt us. As our friendship grew, they invited us out to Shelter Island for a few weeks in the summer of 2001. We happily accepted, got hooked by the place, rented a house the following summer, and in 2003 bought a house—a magical glass, wood, and metal box.

Georgiana, our redoubtable real estate agent on Shelter Island, then sent letters to our neighbors announcing the purchase. The postscript, offering to address their property needs, mattered little compared to the news of a two-father family in a decidedly special house.

At first, I thought Georgiana's gesture was cheeky, but then, after considering how easy she made it for us to meet our neighbors, I was grateful. One early morning, a life-size cow we had bought on a whim was delivered on a flat-bed truck, bound for our side garden. Sarah, from down the road, was out for her daily constitutional and followed the bovine mirage right up the drive. She confessed that she was keen to meet us after receiving the letter, and fell in love with the cow and us on the spot. Then there was Mary, the judge's widow, staunch Democrat and retired schoolteacher who sweetly showed up with a plate of homemade cookies. Owing to her persistence, I registered as a Democrat, my pride at independence abandoned with George W. Bush in the White House.

Robin and Tariq presented themselves one evening, bearing a fine bottle of wine and a copy of Georgiana's letter. Robin said she was an artist with deep roots on Shelter Island, and Tariq, an irresistible Egyptian, was occupied with attending to all needs of Middle Eastern clients. They were taken with the girls and keen to invite us over for supper. In short order we were on their deck enjoying a gourmet meal, with the girls happily devouring hot dogs and watching a video carefully selected for them by our hosts.

In the course of the evening, Robin revealed fragments of her past, centering largely on estrangement from her prominent family. As I was assisting in the kitchen with the dinner dishes, I noticed an enormous portrait of an attractive woman, clearly dating from the 1950s. Robin volunteered that it was her mother and then recounted unhappy tales of her upbringing.

"Why not take it down?" I suggested.

In a flash, we were moving the kitchen table away from the wall, and I had my hands on the gold frame. Robin's delight in so bold a gesture was palpable to us. We then hunted around the house to find a replacement, the empty space almost as intimidating as the portrait itself. Tariq finally produced a calendar-like oil of feluccas on the Nile, its artistic merit of little concern. It went right up on the wall, but the exorcism was incomplete.

On a memorable occasion when Julian's stepfather, Alan—a veteran World War II pilot and "Grandpa" to the girls—was over from England, Robin kindly invited him for a drink. Proud of her studio in the basement of the house, she suggested a tour. On a large board opposite the entrance to the workspace was a prominent sketch titled *Mother*, and across it was meticulously lettered the word *Die*. As though on a royal walkabout, Alan simply glided past it, clucking over other works.

Later that summer we made a tentative date for supper with our new friends but never confirmed the details. In contrast to our structured life in London, we reveled in the informality of our summer. On the appointed day, we didn't take much notice, going off to the beach as usual at 4:00 pm. Upon our return, the phone rang. Our breezy reaction to Robin's distress prompted her to hang up in a huff. I got on my bicycle to go sort out the misunderstanding. As I arrived at their house, the two were about to set out in their car. I gently asked that they not leave. Rather than chronicling the situation, I apologized, assuring them that the mistake was ours. Robin said something about having prepared a rack of lamb and chosen a movie for the girls. I expressed hope that we could get beyond the gaffe. I stood aside, and they drove off.

In the next few days, things seemed to get back on the rails. By the end of the summer, when Tariq asked if he could use our garage to store his vintage Mercedes convertible, we immediately offered it to him.

Over the winter, we received a few calls at odd hours in London from Georgiana. The house alarm had been triggered when Tariq entered the garage. To accommodate our neighbor, we simply switched off the security system so he could readily gain access to his car. We traded humorous e-mails about the untimely alarms and also assured Georgiana that she would no longer be troubled by emergency calls from ADT.

It was soon summer again, and we happily took up our friendship, the rack of lamb incident having receded into the past. Julian received a call from Robin, inviting us for a lobster supper upon my return from the city. An old pal of hers, staying for the weekend, would be joining us, but Tariq was out of town. The evening was merry, with the girls first working on art projects before settling down to yet another good movie. They had happily wolfed down spaghetti as we leisurely savored the lobsters on the broad deck. I still remember the walk home, each of us carrying a little daughter on the starriest of nights.

The next morning, as usual, I drove the girls to Camp Quinipet, waving at the ladies who took their morning constitutionals along the front that ran from Sunset Beach past the Perlman Music campus. Upon my arrival home, I found Julian already at work on his current piece. I then rode off on my bicycle bound for the drugstore to pick up a huge iced coffee and the *New York Times*. I took up my usual position at the tiny plastic table outside the drugstore to work on my little stories. There I sat for a couple of hours, sporting my "do-rag," greeting the occasional passerby, happily reading and writing. At noon, I crossed the street to fetch the mail at the post office before pedaling home.

Julian was not at his usual spot, laboring over his laptop in the garden. The table, made up of two stone slabs salvaged from the sculpture garden of the Museum of Modern Art, was vacant. Rather, he was pacing about the house, appearing both agitated and confused. He went on to explain that Robin had called asking for seventy-two dollars to cover the cost of the lobsters. Initially thinking that she was kidding—not understanding the term "Dutch treat," which she had used— he then realized that she was serious. He had, in fact, just returned from delivering the cash. I had little time to react, with the girls awaiting my arrival at camp to pick them up after their lunch.

When we all returned, Julian and I had a chat, agreeing that there had been no misunderstanding over Robin's request for reimbursement. On my bicycle again, I went to address the matter, despite my predicted nervousness. Soon I was back on the deck of the previous evening's lobster supper trying to understand the cash demand from our hostess, the disinherited heiress.

"You and Julian are so good to us. Just a few nights ago you took us out yet again to supper. I felt that the nature of our relationship just had to change. We are feeling too indebted to you," she explained.

Addressing her aversion to our generosity by righting the perceived imbalance in the wrong direction was puzzling, indeed. Although Robin seemed baffled by my distress, she acknowledged that her timing might have been bad. At that moment, Tariq emerged from the house, refreshed after a long nap. We greeted each other warmly, and I was off.

I reported back to Julian, stressing Robin's awkward recognition of her inappropriate behavior. Ever the peace-maker, I tried to dilute the crassness of her request for pay-ment. Struggling to find a way forward with our neighbors, we decided to invite them for a drink that night. After a few unsuccessful attempts on the phone, I bicycled over to deliver the message in person. Bounding up the few steps onto the deck for a second time that day, I was at the screen door too soon to avoid intruding on a huge row going on between Robin and Tariq. Sheepishly, I asked if my timing was bad.

"Yes," growled Tariq, and I left.

Simultaneous with my arrival back at the house was an e-mail from Robin requesting that I give them notice of future visits to ensure that they would be appropriately dressed for the occasion.

We never saw them again anywhere on the island.

HOME AT LAST

After a four-year assignment with the bank in Hong Kong, I was posted to Tokyo and found myself immediately involved in the calamity attending the Chase purchase of J. P. Morgan. The phone rang one day at my desk, and a woman named Yolan introduced herself as a real estate agent from Princeton. My friend Jack had given her my name, she recounted, as someone who might be interested in moving to Princeton after my foreign assignments had come to an end.

"It never dawned on me, and we're likely to be going on to London from here," I told her.

Undeterred, she pushed on, winkling out my abstract views on property.

Then finally, after faffing about, I came clean. "I would only live at twenty-seven Haslet Avenue," I said, the cinder-block house where I had been at the beck and call of Tamino.

"That's rather specific," commented Yolan.

Over the next months, insightful faxes periodically arrived from her, demonstrating that she had checked out 27 Haslet Avenue and tracked down genuinely worthy properties. I would dutifully respond, acknowledging her effort and taste—which indeed reflected ours—but then remind her that they were just not 27 Haslet Avenue. Even after we moved on to England, the faxes kept coming. Julian and I grew to like this lady, somehow knowing that we would stay in touch, whether a deal was in the offing or not. Then, on a late autumn evening, the telephone rang in our London flat, just south of Hyde Park. It was Yolan saying that Alison's niece, who had been occupying 27 Haslet Avenue, was turning eighty, moving to a retirement community, and putting the house on the market. As it happened, we were about to set off for Christmas in New York, so we arranged a rendezvous in Princeton.

In a matter of days, Julian and the girls were with me in Penn Station on our way down to Princeton. Suddenly standing before us was Ricky, who had shared that magical summer with me decades before, incredulous to hear that we were bound for Alison's house.

Hattie and Tillie were enjoying the train ride, all the more so for having been sent on their own with money to buy snacks. Just as the novelty of it all was wearing thin and the train began slowing to enter the station, Julian blandly commented, "I don't know if I'm quite ready to be buried down a little country lane."

It was not difficult for Yolan to spot us—a two-father, two-daughter family. We piled into her car and went straight to the house; its effect on me was remarkably similar to that very first time so long ago. Those gray blocks seemed to float above the lawn. And the muddy grass did not stop the girls from running off into the garden.

Once inside I spotted the alarm panel I had used incorrectly one night, causing the police to arrive, guns drawn, as I had been warned. The girls were in high spirits, giggling loudly as they fanned out behind the house to take a good look around. Julian was halting, though, as he continued down the entry hall. The girls suddenly spotted the guest house, and Hattie declared that she wanted to keep a horse in it. This was where my mother had stayed the night before I received my PhD, when she was ill with heart disease and needed rest. That her granddaughters—one her namesake—were now checking out that very place, wanting to supplement her memory with a horse, transformed my sudden wistfulness to delight.

"What are these stones?" shouted the girls, pointing to the ground near the back wall of the garden behind the guest house.

I recalled that Alison had had cats buried there. I naughtily jumped onto one marker and started dancing, my memories of Tamino's tyranny rushing back. After calming down, I refreshed the girls' memories about that awful animal, known to them from my stories about him. Looking at each other, the girls seemed to reach telepathic consensus. Such antics were expected of their Baba. It turned out, by the way, that there was no stone for Tamino.

Soon we were heading back to the train. On the platform, with a half-smile, Julian let slip, "I know just where the piano will go."

We now live at 27 Haslet Avenue, but with no horse in the guest house. Fuqi, our pooch from Beijing, goes freely out the dog flap into the garden, in pursuit of squirrels. Tillie occupies Alison's old darkroom upstairs, and Hattie the maid's room atop the kitchen. Julian can often be heard at the piano.

I finally belong.

Acausal Books